A Sense of Mission

A SENSE
OF MISSION

Guidance
from the Gospel of John

by
Albert Curry Winn

The Westminster Press
Philadelphia

Scripture quotations from the Revised Standard Version of the Bible are copyrighted 1946, 1952, © 1971, 1973 by the Division of Christian Education of the National Council of the Churches of Christ in the U.S.A., and are used by permission.

BOOK DESIGN BY ALICE DERR

First edition

Published by The Westminster Press®
Philadelphia, Pennsylvania

PRINTED IN THE UNITED STATES OF AMERICA
9 8 7 6 5 4 3 2 1

Library of Congress Cataloging in Publication Data

Winn, Albert Curry, 1921–
   A sense of mission.

   Includes bibliographical references.
   1. Bible. N.T.-John—Criticism, interpretation, etc. 2. Missions—Biblical teaching. I. Title.
BS2615.2.W55   226'.506   80–28000
ISBN 0–664–24365–7

To my wife,
companion in joy and pain,
who I firmly believe was sent to me by God
as one of his greatest gifts

Contents

Preface

Now and again across the years my mind has been occupied with the use of the little word "send" in the Fourth Gospel. I first worked at it in public in a series of lectures given at the National Ministries Conference of the Presbyterian Church in the United States, in August 1968. Later the entire subject was reworked for the Frank H. Caldwell Lectures given at Louisville Presbyterian Theological Seminary in March 1980.

I wish to express my appreciation to President C. Ellis Nelson of Louisville Presbyterian Theological Seminary for the invitation to deliver the Caldwell Lectures; to my former colleagues on the faculty there, who listened patiently as though an erstwhile administrator and presently working pastor might still have some theological juices in his system; to friends and former students who came from all quarters through a record snowfall to fill the Seminary Chapel and to encourage me beyond all deserving; to Howard Rice, Moderator of the United Presbyterian General Assembly, whose presence as co-lecturer raised the series to a higher level of excitement; and to Frank H. Caldwell himself, present and attentive, former chief, predecessor, model, and continuous inspiration across the years.

No writer can possibly acknowledge his total indebtedness. One of my treasured possessions is a copy of the second edition of *The Fourth Gospel* by Hoskyns and Davey, given to me and inscribed for me by my teacher, Howard Tillman Kuist. Hoskyns and Kuist together taught me to reverence the Fourth Gospel, to discern in it a numinous quality that made me tremble and fascinated me at the same time.

I was well along in my preparation for the Caldwell Lectures when I discovered that my fascination with "send" was shared by a Belgian missionary to South America, José Comblin. In 1974 he had published in Portuguese *O enviado do pai,* which appeared in English dress as *Sent from the Father* (Orbis Books, 1979). The work is so beautiful and sensitive that I have leaned on it heavily in my first chapter and wish at this point to express an indebtedness beyond what is ordinarily conveyed by footnotes.

Finally I owe a special debt to Raymond E. Brown, S.S., whose Sprunt Lectures at Union Seminary in Virginia I had the privilege of hearing just a month before mine were to be delivered. The enthusiasm of the student audience made those lectures a rare event, and I have come to share that enthusiasm even more deeply as I have plowed through Brown's monumental work on John.

Thanks are due to the staff of Second Presbyterian Church in Richmond for "covering" the early morning hours and all-day stints in which the lectures were totally rewritten as a book, and to Grace Winn and Louise English for care and skill in typing.

Introduction

I have written this little book to try to keep my own sense of mission alive, my sense that I have been sent into this world for some high and shining purpose. It is an audacious little book. It assumes a measure of expertise in New Testament studies and in systematic theology, when the Lord knows how difficult it is to be expert in either. It chooses to address, not the specialists, but the generalists—ordinary folk, whether pastors or pew-sitters, who are struggling with me to maintain some sense of mission in a confusing and wrongheaded world.

When I first became a pastor, just after World War II, there was much talk of "mission." That heady word had been brought back from "the foreign field" and cleared for domestic consumption.

We were all missionaries, and the famous quote from Emil Brunner was on everyone's lips: "The church exists by mission as fire exists by burning."

But the decades since have not been hospitable to a sense of mission. For many of us life has become incredibly affluent and sadly meaningless in the midst of the affluence. The American nation seems to have lost any sense of mission and is absorbed with the maintenance of power, the need to be number one at all costs. The churches all too often resemble private clubs which exist for the comfort of their members. And that comfort is often defined as protection from the tides of change that sweep through all other aspects of our culture. Survival, not mission, is our national, ecclesiastical, and personal preoccupation.

So seminarians are having trouble putting together the high idealism that brought them to seminary with the worldly wisdom that shows them how to survive and get ahead in the church. Pastors wonder about their vocation: Are they serving the world's needs or are they running an upper-middle-class institution that exists only to satisfy the needs of its members? The people in the pew, who time and again are genuinely stirred up to do mission in the world, seem to find no outlet and so are vaguely guilty.

Rekindling a sense of mission, then, is a difficult, worthy and essential project. How shall we go about it? I propose a serious Bible study. Scripture is the central flame at which we rekindle what needs rekindling. I propose more particularly a serious study of the Fourth Gospel. And I propose most particularly of all a serious study of how the little word "send" is used in that Gospel. For "mission" is the Latin of "sending," and a sense of mission is precisely a sense of having been sent.

THE RIDDLE OF THE FOURTH GOSPEL

It is at first glance a presumptuous proposal— to study the Fourth Gospel in order to rekindle our sense of mission. For the Fourth Gospel may well be the greatest riddle in the entire New Testament.

For centuries the Fourth Gospel was considered by conservative, orthodox Christians as the "safest" part of Scripture. After all, was it not written by John, one of the twelve apostles, the one closest to and most beloved by Jesus himself? Were not the ancient ecumenical creeds framed in Johannine terms? Was not its "high" Christology a bulwark against all modernisms? Was not the heartthrob of revivalistic Christianity reduced to a single sentence in John 3:16? So, the pioneer missionaries usually translated John first of all, when they succeeded in reducing a newly learned language to writing. The same high evaluation of John appears at the end of Browning's "Bishop Blougram's Apology." After arguing with the bishop, the agnostic writer Gigadibs sails for Australia. And the poet wishes him well in these words:

> —there, I hope,
> By this time he has tested his first plough,
> And studied his last chapter of Saint John.

On the other hand, for the last 150 years of Biblical scholarship, the Gospel of John has been a storm center. Who wrote it? John the son of Zebedee? John the Elder? John Mark? Lazarus? Philip the Evangelist? We might well nominate Martha or Mary Magdalene—as good a case can be made for them. From what Christian community did the writer spring and what community or communities does he or she address? Communities in Ephesus? Syria? Samaria? the Transjordan? What has the author done to the tradition known to us in the other three Gospels? Ignored it? Perverted it? Corrected it? Truly interpreted it? In what sense are the words attributed to Jesus here, so different from his characteristic speech in the other records, really the words of Jesus? How much did the first readers of this Gospel already know about Jesus and why does the writer address them so urgently? What kind of history do we have here? These and many other questions have been warmly and continuously debated.[1]

Whatever else, we are in the presence of a profoundly theological document. We know now that all four Evangelists were theologians, telling their versions of the story of Jesus from very specific theological viewpoints. But when we really open ourselves to the Fourth Gospel, we recognize the appropriateness of that fascinating graffito on a stone found amid the debris of the ancient church of St. John on the hill of Ayasoluk, at the site of ancient Ephesus: "Holy John, evangelist and theologian."[2] The writer of the Fourth Gospel is preeminently "the Theologian."

SEND, SENT, SENT

A significant aspect of John the Theologian's theological method is the repeated use of certain key words. He repeats ordinary words in such fashion that they bear extraordinary theological freight. Such words include light, darkness, spirit, flesh, life, love, glory, witness, judgment, truth, Father, Son, world, work, sign, disciple, know, believe. It has not so often been noticed that there is a third great verb, along with "know" and "believe," the verb "send, sent, sent." This is the great missionary verb, as we remarked above. The Latin, as you may remember from school days, is *mitto, mittere, misi, missus,* from which we get such English words as mission, missionary, commit, commission, and so on.

Actually, in the Greek two synonymous verbs are used for "send": *apostellō* and *pempō.* Rudolf Bultmann, the German Biblical scholar and theologian, suggested that where *apostellō* is used, the stress is on the authority of the one sent; where *pempō* is used, the stress is on the authority of the sender.[3] After a study of all uses of the two verbs in the Fourth Gospel, I do not believe that such a distinction is carried out precisely or consistently. Both verbs mean "send." Both are missionary verbs. And once you observe their pervasive presence in the Fourth Gospel, you are driven to recognize that Gospel as one of the great missionary documents of the New Testament, an obvious place for the rekindling of the flame of your own sense of mission.

THE SHAPE OF OUR STUDY

The broad outlines of our study can now be quickly sketched. We begin by concentrating on Jesus, on his sense of having been sent which permeates John's picture of him. Then we examine the way in which the mission of Jesus is laid upon the community of his disciples, the church. Next we see how each member of the church, each individual disciple, is identified and defined by his or her sense of mission. We then turn to consider the world, into which Jesus, the church, and the disciples are sent. Our next concern is the Paraclete, the Holy Spirit, sent to the church for its mission to the world. Finally we study God in his special role as Sender.

Primarily this book is a Bible study, confined largely to the Fourth Gospel and to the "send, sent, sent" passages which occur in almost every chapter. It could readily serve as a text for a serious adult Bible class. But it is also a programmatic essay for theologians, an appropriate homage to John the Theologian. Among theologians I include not only those few privileged souls who work at theology professionally, but all pastors who want what they preach and how they live to make sense, all seminarians whose faith is truly seeking understanding, all lay persons who wish to be as mature and thoughtful in faith as they are in the affairs of family, business, or society.

In his great little book *The Doctrine of the Holy Spirit* (John Knox Press, 1977), Dutch theologian Hendrikus Berkhof says that we have never permitted the mission of the church to shape the theology of the church. The main outlines of systematic theology were laid down for Catholics in the Middle Ages and for Protestants at the Reformation, and in neither period was the church really missionary. The great missionary movement of the nineteenth century has not yet affected the basic structures of the church's theology.

What is proposed here, in very modest and tentative fashion, is a preliminary outline of a missionary theology—not a special theology for overseas missionaries, but a theology in which the missionary nature of the whole church is central, a theology in which "send, sent, sent" is the principal verb. So Chapter 1 proposes directions in which a missionary Christology, a missionary doctrine of Christ, might move. Chapter 2 does the same for a missionary ecclesiology, a missionary doctrine of the church. Chapter 3 proposes a missionary soteriology, a doctrine of salvation, not full-orbed, but offering some new suggestions as to how one becomes and remains a Christian. Chapter 4 points to a missionary cosmology, not a doctrine of the created order in the old sense, but a missionary understanding of "the world" in the startlingly contemporary Johannine sense. Chapter 5 sketches a missionary pneumatology, a missionary doctrine of the Holy Spirit. And Chapter 6 explores dimensions of a missionary theology proper, a missionary understanding of God the Sender. No one would suggest that the resulting "minisystem" is a complete and adequate systematic theology. It may serve, however, to point up some of the inadequacies of our traditional systems.

We began with the need for recovering and maintaining our own sense of mission. If such a sense of mission is to endure in the final cataclysmic decades of this century, it cannot rest on catchy mottos and nifty illustrations. It must be Biblically based and thought out in some systematic theological fashion. Let's have at it.

1. Jesus: The One Who Was Sent

> You know me, and you know where I come from? But I have not come of my own accord; he who sent me is true, and him you do not know. I know him, for I come from him, and he sent me. (John 7:28–29)
>
> If God were your Father, you would love me, for I proceeded and came forth from God; I came not of my own accord, but he sent me. (John 8:42)[4]

The first step in maintaining or getting a sense of mission for oneself is to feel the sweep and power of Jesus' own sense of mission. The Johannine Jesus does not appear on the scene as a volunteer. He is on no self-appointed rescue effort. He lives and speaks and acts out of a profound sense of mission, a conviction that he has been sent.

The above texts are the merest sample of sayings that mark almost every chapter of the Fourth Gospel, in which Jesus says over and over and over again that he has been sent. He refers to himself constantly as the one whom God has sent (John 5:38; 6:29; 10:36; 17:3). He refers even more constantly to God as the Sender (John 4:34; 5:23, 24, 37; 6:38, 39, 44, 57; 7:16, 18, 28, 29; 8:16, 18, 26,

29; 9:4; 11:42; 12:49; 13:20; 14:24; 15:21; 16:5; 17:8, 21, 23, 25). The sense of having been sent into the world by God lies at the very core of Jesus' self-understanding.

We intend to deal in this chapter with most of the sayings just referred to, and others as well. But before we attempt an analysis of them, there are two preliminary questions we must face. How is all this Johannine material related to the earlier tradition in Matthew, Mark, and Luke? And how is it related to the Gnostic redeemer myth?

RELATION TO THE EARLIER TRADITION

The Johannine emphasis on Jesus' sense of mission is not totally unrelated to the tradition we find in the Synoptic Gospels. It is my observation that very little in John is totally unrelated to the earlier tradition—not that the writer of John had read Matthew and Mark and Luke, but that he was clearly familiar with the tradition they represent.

The Synoptic Jesus has a sense of having been sent. In Mark this comes to light almost incidentally, in a saying about the humility and importance of children: to receive a child is to receive Jesus, and to receive Jesus is to receive the One who sent him:

Whoever receives one such child in my name receives me; and whoever receives me, re-

ceives not me but him who sent me. (Mark
9:37)

This saying is reproduced almost verbatim in
Luke:

> Whoever receives this child in my name re-
> ceives me, and whoever receives me receives
> him who sent me. (Luke 9:48)

Matthew adapts the saying to the great mission
charge to the apostles, and the child is replaced by
the missionaries:

> He who receives you receives me, and he
> who receives me receives him who sent me.
> (Matt. 10:40)

Luke does something similar in the mission
charge to the seventy, stressing the negative cor-
ollary: to reject the missionaries is to reject Jesus,
and to reject Jesus is to reject the One who sent
him:

> He who hears you hears me, and he who
> rejects you rejects me, and he who rejects me
> rejects him who sent me. (Luke 10:16)

Other indications of Jesus' sense of having been
sent peep around the corners in Matt. 15:24, Luke
4:18 and 43. What John has done is to take this
theme which he found in the tradition and make it
central, foundational to his Christology.

All four Gospels are Christological documents.
Even in Mark, a central question is: Who is this
Jesus? (Mark 1:27; 2:7; 4:41; 6:2–3, 14–16; 8:27–29;

15:39). The answers to the question are familiar to us: the Christ (1:1; 8:29; 9:41; 14:61; 15:32), the Son of God (1:1, 11; 3:11; 5:7; 9:7; 14:61; 15:39), the Holy One of God (1:24), the Son of man (2:10, 28; 8:31, 38; 9:9, 12, 31; 10:33, 45; 13:26; 14:21, 41, 62), John the baptizer risen from the dead (6:14, 16; 8:28), Elijah (6:15; 8:28), one of the prophets (6:15; 8:28), Son of David (10:47, 48; 11:10; 12:35–37), King of the Jews (15:2, 9, 12, 18, 26), King of Israel (15:32). Overlaid on all these questions and all these titles is Mark's well-known "Messianic secret": the writer and the readers know from the start who Jesus is; so do the unclean spirits; but the disciples do not know until Peter makes his confession in 8:29; Jesus charges them to keep it secret and makes an open claim only at the very end, under questioning by the high priest in 14:62.

John ignores the "Messianic secret" altogether. Jesus makes open claims from the start. Yet John is familiar with the whole array of Marcan titles and uses most of them: the Christ (John 1:17, 41; 4:25–26, 29; 7:26, 27, 31, 41, 42; 9:22; 10:24; 11:27; 12:34; 17:3; 20:31), the Son of God (1:18, 34, 49; 3:16, 17, 18; 5:25; 10:36; 11:27; 19:7; 20:30), the Holy One of God (6:69), the Son of man (1:51; 3:13, 14; 5:27; 6:27, 53, 62; 8:28; 9:35; 12:23, 34; 13:31), the prophet (4:19; 6:14; 7:40, 52; 9:17), Son of David (7:42), King of the Jews (18:33, 39; 19:3, 14, 15, 19, 21), King of Israel (1:49; 12:13).

But in John the central question is not so much, Who is Jesus? What is the appropriate title for him? as, Where does he come from? (John 1:46; 3:2; 6:42; 7:27, 41–42; 9:16, 29; 16:30; 19:9) and, Where is he going? (7:33–36; 8:21–22; 13:3, 33, 36; 14:2–6, 12, 19, 28; 16:5–7, 16; 20:17). And the answer to this central question is no longer a noun, but a verb. Jesus is the one who has been sent from the Father and who returns to the Father. That, more than any title or set of titles, constitutes the core of his identity.

It is this characteristic of John's account that raises the question of Gnosticism in its sharpest form.

RELATION TO THE GNOSTIC REDEEMER MYTH

At the beginning of the Christian era, Greek thought and Greek language were sweeping into the world of the Middle East. But with equal force the currents of Oriental religions were sweeping across the Greek world. In the wild riot of syncretisms that resulted, there emerged a religion or a group of closely related religions, to which we have given the name "Gnosticism." It was a religion of salvation, salvation by *gnōsis*, knowledge.

In the various schools of Gnosticism there was an infinite variety of things to be taught and known, but a central thread could be clearly identified: the myth of the redeemer who was sent into the world. To the Gnostic teachers the world was a place of utter darkness. Its very materiality—its being matter—was by definition evil. Trapped in matter were souls that belonged to another world. Trapped in darkness were sparks of celestial light. This world was far, far removed from the God of light, who in fact did not create it; the creator was an evil figure, like the world he created, flawed and ignorant. Souls attempting to escape back to the God of light had to face gate after gate, guarded by the terrible Archons. But God sent a Messenger of light, an alien Person, down through all the gates, into the darkness of this world, to free the scattered bits of light. The redeemer's appearance in the world brought about a great separation between light and darkness. Those who were of the light, themselves alien to the world, recognized the messenger of light. Those who were of the darkness did not. With the enlightened ones, the ones "in the know," the redeemer escaped back upward to the realm of light.

There is no question in my mind that the Fourth Gospel and the Gnostic redeemer myth belong to the same universe of discourse. When we read that eternal life consists in knowing—knowing the true God and the one he has sent (John 17:3); that the redeemer's followers are not of the world, even as he is not of the world (17:16); that he will take them to himself, that where he is, there they may be also (14:3); that the one who comes from above is above all, while the one who is of the earth belongs to the earth and speaks of the earth

(3:31); that light has come into the world, and people loved darkness rather than light, because their deeds were evil (3:19)—we are reading statements to which Gnostics could readily vibrate.

They belong to the same universe of discourse, but what is the connection? Bultmann[5] proposed that the Fourth Gospel originated in an environment where an early form of Gnosticism was already flourishing. Its author adopted Gnostic vocabulary and concepts, recognizing their power, but used them in order to attack and refute Gnosticism. The problem with this thesis is that we have no clear evidence of the existence of an early Gnosticism at the time the Gospel was written. All the documents that clearly tell us about Gnosticism come from the following century.

With encyclopedic scholarship and dazzling imagination, Raymond E. Brown has reconstructed a different story of the Johannine community.[6] They were a group of Christians who did not accept the authority of the twelve apostles, but claimed the authority of the Beloved Disciple, and above all of the Paraclete, the Holy Spirit dwelling in their midst. In conflict with the Jews and other groups they developed the "high" Christology of the Fourth Gospel. The Johannine epistles show us that a split occurred in the community. The seceding group interpreted the Fourth Gospel in ways congenial to Gnosticism, and eventually became Gnostics, carrying the Gospel with them into Gnostic circles.[7] The group that stood with the writer of the Johannine epistles interpreted the Fourth Gospel in ways congenial with mainline Christianity, and eventually joined the churches of apostolic origin. It was through them that the Fourth Gospel passed into the life of the church catholic.

However we account for it, a certain affinity exists between the Fourth Gospel and the Gnostic redeemer myth. What is more important is to mark the significant differences between them.

It is easy to see what a thoroughly Gnostic Christology would look like. Jesus would be the divine Messenger from the realm of light. He would visit this world, not as a naturalized citizen, but with an alien visa. As a noncitizen he would not share the human predicament as we know it. He would only seem to be human. As pure light he could not share the darkness of our ignorance, our pain, our shame, our mortality. He would not really be one of us. To use the ancient term, a Gnostic Jesus would be "docetic."

We know, of course, from early Christian writings that just such a docetic Christology did emerge and had to be stoutly combated. We know, too, that vast numbers of Christians today—"good, Bible-believing Christians"—are unwittingly Gnostics, embracing a thoroughly docetic Christology, feeling that the height of piety is to remove Jesus as far from our humanity as possible.

Let us be crystal clear about this. John is antidocetic in his Christology. Even though John talks about Jesus who came from the Father and returns to the Father (John 3:13, 31; 13:1; 14:1–2; 16:28); even though he stresses the knowledge of Jesus up to the borders of omniscience (1:48; 4:17–18; 6:15, 64; 13:1), John's Jesus is a citizen of this world, he is one of us.

The Johannine Jesus had a body that could bleed (John 19:34). He could be weary (4:6) and thirsty (19:28). He spat (9:6). He performed menial tasks like washing feet (13:4–5). He requested information: "Where have you laid him?" (11:34). He groaned and wept at the tomb of Lazarus (11:33, 35, 38). His spirit was deeply troubled (12:27; 13:21). He loved (11:5; 13:23; 20:2). Two two-word sentences forever exempt the Fourth Gospel from the charge of docetism. One, at the tomb of Lazarus: "Jesus wept." The other, on the cross: "I thirst." John is utterly serious when he says at the outset, in his Prologue: "The Word became flesh and dwelt among us" (1:14).

Let's get our bearings. We have said that the verb "send" is the center of the Christological concentration of the Fourth Gospel; that this Christology has its roots in the earlier tradition, though it is not as explicit or central there; that this Christology offered an opening for dialogue with the Gnostic religion; that it was nevertheless clearly and categorically antidocetic. It now remains for us to analyze this Christology, to see how it works and whether it can give us, being who we are, living when and where we live, a deeper understanding of the ineffable mystery of who Jesus is.

THE ANALYSIS

1. As a part of his sense-of-having-been-sent, Jesus acknowledges that *his will is not his own, but God's.*

> My food is to do the will of him who sent me. (John 4:34)

> I seek not my own will, but the will of him who sent me. (5:30)

> For I have come down from heaven, not to do my own will, but the will of him who sent me. (6:38)

> He who sent me is with me; he has not left me alone, for I always do what is pleasing to him. (8:29)

This is not a grudging submission to the will of God, but a glad embrace of it. He has an appetite for it, and it sustains him; he feeds on it; it is the root of his companionship with God.

2. It follows that *Jesus' words are not his own, but God's.*

> My teaching is not mine, but his who sent me; if any [one's] will is to do his will, he shall

know whether the teaching is from God or whether I am speaking on my own authority. He who speaks on his own authority seeks his own glory; but he who seeks the glory of him who sent him is true, and in him there is no falsehood. (John 7:16–18)

When you have lifted up the Son of man, then you will know that I am he, and that I do nothing on my own authority but speak thus as the Father taught me. (8:28)

For I have not spoken on my own authority; the Father who sent me has himself given me commandment what to say and what to speak. (12:49)

The word which you hear is not mine but the Father's who sent me. (14:24)

I have given them the words which thou gavest me, and they have received them and know in truth that I came from thee; and they have believed that thou didst send me. (17:8)

It is not that the words of the Sender have been deposited with the Sent One as a possession which he may keep and dole out upon occasion. The Sent One's mouth is filled with the Sender's words, because his ear is filled with them. Speaking depends on *hearing*.

I can do nothing on my own authority; as I hear, I judge. (John 5:30)

I have much to say about you and much to judge; but he who sent me is true, and I declare to the world what I have heard from him. (8:26)

But now you seek to kill me, a man who has told you the truth which I heard from God. (8:40)

He who is of God hears the words of God. (8:47)

All that I have heard from my Father I have made known to you. (15:15)

The Johannine Jesus can speak the words of God, not only because he is radically attentive at each moment to what God is saying, but because he *knows* God.

He who sent me is true, and him you do not know. I know him, for I come from him, and he sent me. (John 7:28–29)

You have not known him; I know him. If I said, I do not know him, I should be a liar like you; but I do know him and I keep his word. (8:55)

O righteous Father, the world has not known thee, but I have known thee; and these know that thou hast sent me. (17:25)

It is important to note that this knowing is no more a permanent possession of the Sent One than the hearing. It is not a deposit of knowledge, objective, owned, controlled. It gives the Sent One no advantage or power over the Sender. He does not claim to know the Sender as the Sender knows himself.[8] His knowledge of God is what is given with coming from God, being sent by God, keeping God's word. It is a missionary knowledge of God. It is enough to enable him to speak God's words and not his own.

3. Jesus declares that *his works are not his own, but God's.*

> My food is to do the will of him who sent me, and to accomplish his work. (John 4:34)

> The works which the Father has granted me to accomplish, these very works which I am doing, bear me witness that the Father has sent me. (5:36)

> We must work the works of him who sent me, while it is day; night comes when no one can work. (9:4)

The Fourth Gospel does not record as many of Jesus' works as the earlier Gospels do. Those works which are recorded are often called signs, pointers (John 2:11; 4:54; 20:30). To what do they point? To the Sender, whose works they really are. Every sign, every work of Jesus, is to be interpreted by these words:

> My Father is working still, and I am working. . . . The Son can do nothing of his own accord, but only what he sees the Father doing; for whatever he does, that the Son does likewise. (John 5:17, 19)

4. Finally, as a part of his sense-of-having-been-sent, Jesus acknowledges that *his very life depends on the Sender.*

> As the living Father sent me, and I live because of the Father, so he who eats me will live because of me. (John 6:57)

As his words are no permanent possession, but are given to him moment by moment as he continually hears; as his works are done moment by moment as he watches what the Father is doing, so his life is drawn moment by moment from the Father.

TRANSPARENCY AND GLORY

It is impossible to read the sayings in which the Johannine Jesus expounds his sense-of-having-been-sent without noticing a profound mystery. The more humble the sayings are, the more majestic they are. Every assertion of utter humility is at one and the same time an assertion of majesty!

I was not sent to do my own will—humility! Therefore, I do the will of God—majesty!

I was not sent to speak my own words—humility! Therefore, I speak the words of God—majesty!

I was not sent to do my own works—humility! Therefore, I do the works of God—majesty!

I was not sent to live my own life—humility! Therefore, my life is the life of God in
your midst—majesty!

The Johannine Christology is a Christology of
transparency. That is Paul Tillich's term and a
good one. Tillich says that a final revelation—the
decisive, fulfilling, unsurpassable revelation, that
which is the criterion of all other revelations—
must be transparent. The medium of the revelation must call no attention to itself, direct all attention to what is revealed. This, says Tillich, con-
demns a Jesus-centered religion and theology.[9]
We are not called to be admirers of the human
Jesus, of his sterling character and heroic quali-
ties. The characteristically German fascination
with Jesus as a figure of titanic proportions, hid-
den from us by the mists of tradition, was the
wrong track. Albert Schweitzer says of David
Friedrich Strauss's first *Life of Jesus,* "Behind
the billowy mists of legend we caught from time
to time a momentary glimpse of the gigantic
figure of Jesus."[10] And Schweitzer summarizes
his own reconstruction with the words: "There is
silence all around. The Baptist appears, and cries:
'Repent, for the Kingdom of Heaven is at hand.'
Soon after that comes Jesus, and in the knowledge that He is the coming Son of Man lays hold
of the wheel of the world to set it moving on that
last revolution which is to bring all ordinary history to a close. It refuses to turn, and He throws

Himself upon it. Then it does turn; and crushes Him. . . . The wheel rolls onward, and the mangled body of the one immeasurably great Man, who was strong enough to think of Himself as the spiritual ruler of mankind and to bend history to His purpose, is hanging upon it still. That is His victory and His reign."[11] Not so, says Tillich. Jesus is the final revelation because of "the continuous self-surrender of Jesus who is Jesus to Jesus who is the Christ."[12] Fascination with a titanic Jesus is Jesusolatry. Jesus, according to John, points away from himself to the One who sent him. He is utterly transparent. As a revealer of God he lets all the light through. John 12:44–45 is a definitive statement of transparency: "He who believes in me, believes not in me but in him who sent me. And he who sees me sees him who sent me."

The Johannine Christology is also a Christology of *glory*. The Fourth Gospel is a continuous transfiguration narrative. What happens in the other Gospels in a special mountaintop theophany (Matt. 17:1–8; Mark 9:2–8; Luke 9:28–36) happens continuously in John: the glory of God shines through the humble, transparent humanity of Jesus.

Jesus becomes the test of whether we honor God: "He who does not honor the Son does not honor the Father who sent him" (John 5:23). God himself witnesses in Jesus' behalf: "And the Father who sent me has himself borne witness to me" (5:37; see also 8:18). There is no knowledge of God apart from faith in Jesus: "His voice you have never heard, his form you have never seen; and you do not have his word abiding in you, for you do not believe him whom he has sent" (5:37–38). What the Sender requires is faith in the Sent One: "This is the work of God, that you believe in him whom he has sent" (6:29; see also 11:42; 17:8, 21, 23).

Jesus is the Way: "No one comes to the Father, but by me" (John 14:6). Jesus is the Truth: "He who seeks the glory of him who sent him is true, and in him there is no falsehood" (7:18). Jesus is the Life: "For as the Father has life in himself, so he has granted the Son also to have life in himself" (5:26). The great "I Am's" of the Fourth Gospel follow naturally: "I am the bread of life" (6:35). "I am the light of the World" (8:12). "I am the door" (10:7). "I am the good shepherd" (10:11). "I am the true vine" (15:1). "Before Abraham was, I am" (8:58).[13]

There is, in the end, a unity between the Sender and the Sent One. "I and the Father are one" (John 10:30). "He who has seen me has seen the Father" (14:9). "I am in the Father and the Father in me" (14:10, 11; 17:21). This unity is not a reduction to identity, not the static unity of an equation between two nouns. It is a verbal unity, the dynamic unity that lies at the depths of the verb "send."

Just as we can say nothing that is too lowly for Jesus, the poor, suffering, impotent, transparent human being, so we can make no claim too great for him. In Thomas Kelly's words, which generations of Christians have sung:

> The highest place that heaven affords
> Is his, is his by right.

DEVELOPING A MISSIONARY CHRISTOLOGY

If theologians in our day, under the guidance of John the Theologian, should set out to rethink the Doctrine of Christ in a missionary way, where would it lead? It would lead, I think, to a reevaluation of the Formula of Chalcedon, which has provided the framework for Christological debate ever since the fifth century. It would not lead to a "lower" Christology than Chalcedon's. Some may even call it "higher." But it would be a Christology of verbs instead of a Christology of nouns.

After centuries of debate, which, as we said earlier, was fought out on Johannine turf, the Council of Chalcedon formulated the results in the familiar terms: "two natures in one person." The "natures" of Christ were *things*, nouns: his humanity and his Godhead, or deity. He is "consubstantial"—of the same substance, another *thing* —with the Father as to his deity, consubstantial with us as to his humanity. He is "perfect"—complete—in his deity and in his humanity. These two things are not to be confused or altered, divided or separated, but held together and preserved in the unity of one Person.

It is my conviction that we should treat the Formula of Chalcedon with great respect and with considerable gratitude for its function as a bulwark against heresy across the centuries. But we must also be honest about the problems that are its legacy to the church.

One problem is that the two natures often assume greater reality than the one person; we are forever engaged in doublethink about Jesus. John Calvin himself in his chapter on "How the Two Natures of the Mediator Make One Person" sorted out the sayings and descriptions of Jesus that he found in Scripture into four piles. Here, he said, the human nature is spoken of. And here the divine nature is spoken of. Here both natures together are spoken of. And occasionally there is a *communicatio idiomatum:* what is proper to the human nature is ascribed to the divine and vice versa.[14] One wants to ask: Where is the "one Person" spoken of? What happened to Jesus in all this?

In the ongoing saga of American fundamentalism, a key test question is: "Do you believe in the deity of Christ?" One of the "natures" is now the object of faith! From reading the Bible one would rather suppose that the "one Person," Christ himself, is the object of faith. This displacement of faith can be understood when we see that it points to the most basic problem with the Chalcedonian Formula: the two natures are in competition with each other! At least in the mind of many Christians, the more humanity, the less deity; and the more deity, the less humanity. So, "believing in the deity of Christ" is a defense against an emphasis on his humanity that would obliterate his Godhead. It often leads, however, to a naive docetism, as we saw above, that gives us a totally unscriptural Christ.

A Christology based on John the Theologian, a verbal Christology built around Jesus' sense-of-having-been-sent, might escape this dilemma. The humility and the majesty, the transparency and the glory, the humanity and the deity, if you will, are not here in competition. The more humble Jesus is, the more majestic he is; the more transparent, the more glorious; the more one he is with us, the more one he is with the Father. We are not invited to believe in two things, two natures, but in one Person, in the One whom God has sent. And in fulfilling his vocation as the Sent One, Jesus becomes ever more humble, ever more majestic; ever more transparent, ever more glorious; ever more one of us, ever more one with the Father.

Another problem bequeathed us by Chalcedon concerns the *imitatio Christi*, the imitation of Christ, following his example, becoming like him. Can we really follow the Christ of Chalcedon, a heraldic figure, with a divine nature and a human nature that can no more mix than oil and water and cannot be separated either? We are not like that and how can we follow or imitate that?

The Johannine Jesus is imitable. The cosmic language (so close to Gnosticism) seems to say he is not. What have we to do with coming from above and going where our enemies cannot follow, coming down from heaven and returning to the Father? In a notable passage, John shows how this cosmic drama can be first earthed, then imitated. Chapter 13 begins with the cosmic: Jesus knows that his mysterious hour has come, that he has come from God and is going to God (vs. 1–4); he proceeds then to enact the cosmic drama in earthly terms. He rises from supper and lays aside his garments. He girds himself with a towel, takes a basin, and washes his disciples' feet. Then he takes his garments again and resumes his seat. The shape of the earthly deed, a humble, transparent action on behalf of others, is an exact imitation of the shape of the cosmic deed. He speaks:

> Do you know what I have done to you? You call me Teacher and Lord; and you are right, for so I am. If I then, your Lord and Teacher, have washed your feet, you also ought to wash one another's feet. For I have given you an example, that you also should do as I have done to you. Truly, truly, I say to you, a servant is not greater than his master; nor is he who is sent greater than he who sent him. (John 13:12–16)

The essence of Jesus' sense-of-having-been-sent does not lie in the cosmic framework of heavenly descent and ascent. It lies in his mission to meet the human needs of people in this world. And he expressly commands us to embark on the same mission and so to become imitators of him.

It will be a distant imitation, to be sure, marred by our sinfulness, but nonetheless a real one. We can have a sense that God has a mission for us in this world. In a remote but real way, we can will to do God's will. We can speak God's words. We can do God's works. We can draw our life from the living God. We can even experience something like transparency and glory.

But that takes us into the territory of the next two chapters, where we shall analyze the "sentness" of the church and of its individual members.

2. The Church: Sent by Jesus

As the Father has sent me, even so I send you.
(John 20:21)

The setting, appropriately, is Easter evening, the doors being shut where the disciples were, for fear of their enemies. Through shut doors Jesus comes, stands in their midst, blesses them with his peace, shows them his hands and side. Then he says: "As the Father has sent me, even so I send you." In that one powerful sentence, Jesus joins the mission of the church to his mission, moves all the enormous freight of his mission, which we examined in the preceding chapter, onto the back of the church. If the sense of having been sent defines who Jesus is, from henceforth it must define what the church is. Christology must determine ecclesiology.

The word "church" does not occur in John, and figures as formidable as Bultmann and Eduard

Schweizer have maintained that Johannine ecclesiology is so minimal as to be virtually nonex-
istent. But everywhere there are signs of a community from which the Gospel sprang and to
which it is addressed. The idea of an individualistic
religion with no supportive community—"I come
to the garden alone"—is a very modern invention,
and quite unthinkable in the Old Testament tradition in which John clearly stands. The Old Testament images of the flock and the vine, used in
John 10 and John 15, reflect the idea of a people
of God. And the "you" (plural) of our text, with its
context of the outpouring of the Holy Spirit and
the power of the keys, is sufficient to indicate that
we are dealing at this point with the church.

THE SENT PEOPLE OF CHRIST

What distinguishes the church from the world,
from other groupings of people or other institutions in the world? Many things, perhaps, but for
the Fourth Gospel the church is primarily distinguished from everything else by its mission. As
Jesus is unique because God sent him into the
world, so the church is unique because Christ
sends it into the world. As his mission is the basis
for Jesus' self-understanding, so its mission must
be the basis for the church's self-understanding.

It follows that the distinctive marks of the Sent
One, which we analyzed in the preceding chapter,

should be the distinctive marks of the Sent People. That is what is involved when we said that Christology must determine ecclesiology.

1. As the Sent One's will was not his own, but God's, so *the Sent People's will is not their own, but Christ's.* The church must learn to say: "I seek not my own will but the will of him who sent me" (John 5:30).

In a truly missionary church, the function of church courts, conferences, conventions, or other deliberative bodies is not to get the will of my party voted, nor yet a compromise between my party and your party, but to determine, if we can, the will of Christ.

This marks the end of all notions that the church should "speak for its members," take the position on issues that is most congenial to the majority of its constituency. A missionary church, which knows itself to be sent into the world by Christ, will seek Christ's will. That may well be difficult to determine, but we shall never determine it if we are seeking something else or something less.

2. As the Sent One's words were not his own, but God's, so *the Sent People's words are not their own, but Christ's.* The church must learn to say: "My teaching is not mine, but his who sent me" (John 7:16).

The church's speaking depends as Christ's did on constant, attentive *hearing.* The existence in the church of a closed canon of Scripture is neces-

sary, but problematic. Because we possess what
has already been heard from God, because we can
put it in our pockets or pocketbooks, thump it,
parade it, we fall under the illusion that the time
of listening for a fresh and current word of Christ
is gone. We take comfort in the words of the Westminster Divines: "Those former ways of God's
revealing his will unto his people being now
ceased."[15] But God did not become a deaf-mute
with the closing of the canon. The sermon addressed to the Mayflower Pilgrims is more to the
point: "The Lord hath more truth and light yet to
break forth out of his holy Word." When the
preacher clicks on the little lectern light and says
tremulously and a bit uncertainly, "Listen for the
word of God," she or he is calling upon Christ's
sent people to be just as attentive to what he may
say to them in this day as Christ was attentive to
the Father in his day.

The church speaks the word of Christ because
it *knows* Christ. Just as Jesus' knowledge of the
One who sent him was not an objective knowledge
of God as God knows himself, but a missionary
knowledge arising from being sent by God, so the
church's knowledge of Christ gives it no control
over Christ. The church does not have Christ
"down pat." It cannot fathom his mystery, answer all the questions that may be asked about
him. It does know that Christ has loved it, redeemed it, and sent it into the world to speak his
words. Here is the charter for the kind of modest,

"confessional" theology of which H. Richard Niebuhr loved to speak.

It has never been a sign of health in the church when the function of preaching was downgraded. There are surely other forms of communication, but it is through "the folly of what we preach" (I Cor. 1:21) that the church now and again hears Christ and speaks the word of Christ to the world. Let us make sure that we proclaim the words of Christ, and not ourselves. And let us let the words be their own authority, not our robes, or stoles, or diplomas.

3. As the Sent One's works were not his own, but God's, so *the Sent People's works are not their own, but Christ's.* The church must learn to say: "My food is to do the will of him who sent me, and to accomplish his work" (John 4:34).

Just as our constant temptation is to take Christ's words and make them our words, so they are no longer addressed to us, but rather possessed by us, so we are tempted to take Christ's work and make it our work. It is no longer work in which we are invited to join, but work for which we have assumed the primary responsibility. Therefore we set the goals, determine the objectives, prioritize them, devise the strategies, and impose the timetables. Behold the demonic element in the whole church management movement. There is another process involved, it seems to me, when the Sent People of Christ do the works of the One who sent them:

We serve humankind
  by discerning what God is doing in the
  world
  and joining him in his work.
We risk disagreement and error
  when we try to say what God is doing here
  and now.
But we find guidance in God's deeds in the past
  and his promises for the future,
  as they are witnessed to in Scripture.
We affirm that the Lord is at work,
  especially in events and movements
  that free people by the gospel
  and advance justice, compassion, and
  peace.[16]

There is promise here, as well as demand. If the works remain Christ's works, and Christ retains the responsibility for them, then Christ's Sent People can be free from the strain and nervousness and guilt that mark so much "church work." Jesus was remarkably free from those things, and we have been sent as he was sent.

Evangelism is often an area of strain, nervousness, and guilt. Jesus was content to leave the evangelistic results of his proclamation in the Father's hand. "No one can come to me unless the Father who sent me draws him" (John 6:44). Perhaps the Sent People can learn to leave evangelistic results in the hand of the Sent One. No one will join us unless Christ, who sends us, draws him or her.

4. As the Sent One's very life depended on the

Sender, so *the Sent People draw their life from Christ.*

John recognized, of course, that the Eucharist is the great sign that points to the dependence of the church on Christ for its very life. He does an interesting thing. He moves the Eucharist out of the privacy of the upper room. He delivers his eucharistic teaching in connection with the very public event of the feeding of the five thousand.

"Labor . . . for the food which endures to eternal life, which the Son of man will give to you" (John 6:27). "I am the bread of life; he who comes to me shall not hunger, and he who believes in me shall never thirst" (6:35). "I am the living bread which came down from heaven; if any one eats of this bread, he will live forever; and the bread which I shall give for the life of the world is my flesh" (6:51). "As the living Father sent me, and I live because of the Father, so he who eats me will live because of me" (6:57).

The use of the word "flesh" here is clearly anti-Gnostic. The life which the church draws from Christ does not come from the quick transit of a heavenly being through our darkened world. It comes from the life he lived among us in the flesh, the incarnate life on our map and our calendar. Jesus can give life to the church which he sends into the world because he himself was sent into the world and lived out his life there in the flesh.

The church, too, is enfleshed, not at all immaterial and invisible. It is an institution, and institutions tend to have a life of their own. This is a problem we must live with, because a noninstitutional church is as Gnostic as a nonincarnate Jesus. It is a question of relative importance. Which shall have the priority: the church's institutional life, its buildings and budget? or the life which the church draws from Christ who sends it into the world? Whether a church is missionary or not is often decided just at this point.

TRANSPARENCY AND GLORY

In sum, if the Sent One was *transparent*, so must the Sent People be. The church should not call attention to itself. It should not advertise its own institutional excellencies—"the largest organ east of Salt Lake City." It should not trumpet its own virtues—"the friendliest church in town." It should not point to its theological correctness—"holding fast the faith once for all delivered to the saints." Indeed, a truly missionary church makes no ethical claims to be better than the world. It admits and rejoices in the existence of exemplary humanists, exemplary devotees of other faiths. It knows that God loves the world, as well as the church (John 3:16).

A truly missionary church does not seek its own will, speak its own words, perform its own works, live its own life. Its election is the election of a window. It is true to its election the less it claims

for itself and the more it claims for the One who
sent it.

Does the missionary church also have a *glory*
as Jesus had? It is muted, but it is there. Just as
Jesus, the Sent One, became the test of whether
people honored God who sent him (John 5:23), the
test of their faith in God (6:29), so the church,
sinful, corrupt, imperfect as it is, becomes the test
of whether people will honor Christ who sends it,
the test of their faith in Christ. The Lucan saying
sums up the thrust of a whole collection of Johannine sayings: "He who hears you hears me, and he
who rejects you rejects me" (Luke 10:16). Because
Christ has chosen to be known in the world
through a community of ordinary, sinful people,
to despise the church is to despise Christ.

Christ's glory rested in a oneness with the One
who sent him. Can the church claim a oneness
with Christ? Certainly not a reduction to identity,
not the static unity of an equation between two
nouns. We dare not say: "The church is Christ."
That would obliterate the distinction between the
body and the Head, the bride and the Bridegroom,
the redeemed and the Redeemer. But there is a
verbal unity, a dynamic unity that lies at the
depths of the verb "send." The church is Christ's
body. Replacing the body of flesh he had on earth,
it is the vehicle in which he chooses to be recognized, to speak, to work, to suffer. "Saul, Saul,"
said the voice to the church's great persecu-
tor, "why do you persecute me?" (Acts 9:4). That

is the glory of the church.

And it is the glory of the visible church. Let us have done with the Gnostic notion of an invisible church up there somewhere, free from spot or blemish or any such thing. That is, according to Ephesians, the eschatological destiny of the church (Eph. 5:27). But the only church we know now, and the church to which the glorious mission of Christ has been entrusted, is just this visible, spotted, blemished church of which we are a part. "Take good note," Karl Barth once wrote, "that a parson who does not believe that in this congregation of his, including those men and women, old wives and children, Christ's congregation exists, does not believe at all in the existence of the Church."[17]

DEVELOPING A MISSIONARY ECCLESIOLOGY

The doctrine of the church which we have found in John seems to me to call for some revisions of our conventional ecclesiology.

The time-honored *notae ecclesiae*, the marks of the church, are the preaching of the word and the administration of the sacraments. Says Calvin: "Wherever we find the word of God purely preached and heard, and the sacraments adminis- tered according to the institution of Christ, there, it is not to be doubted, is a Church of God."[18] I have no more quarrel with those signs than with the Formula of Chalcedon. But if we are on the right track in these studies, then surely the pre-eminent mark of the church is engagement in mission to the world. If mission defines who Christ is, and if Christ sends us as he was sent, then mission defines who we are. We can preach the word and celebrate the sacraments in all solemnity, propriety, and purity, but if we are doing nothing to speak the words of God and to do the works of God in the world, if we have no concern for liberation, justice, compassion, and peace, can we claim the name of church? I think not.

The big revision must be in our practice, and this is the burden of this chapter, and indeed of the entire book. The churches that ministers serve, that lay people are members of, that seminarians aspire to serve, are only marginally in mission. All too often they are private religious clubs. They offer religious diversions instead of golf and tennis, but otherwise they resemble all too closely the local country club.

Few clubs can stand much diversity in their membership. Usually the members are all of one race, with perhaps a token minority member or two in this enlightened age. And it is important for those minority members to conform with respect to other important matters such as social class, economic bracket, and general political outlook. How often this same homogeneity characterizes our local congregations!

Now comes the Church Growth movement and

testifies that it is precisely such homogeneous congregations that grow most rapidly, like attracting like. The homogeneity is not to be regretted, but prized. I do not question their statistics. And I do not make a virtue of shrinking churches, claiming that they are necessarily more courageous and faithful. I simply ask: What is it that is growing: a church? or a club?

Clubs are often held together by personal admiration, by networks of dominance and dependency. The most difficult and the most valuable pages of Bonhoeffer's *Life Together* are those in which he discusses this phenomenon, which he calls *seelisch* ("soulish") or "direct" relationships. Such relationships subject others to ourselves, instead of subjecting ourselves to others. They bind others to ourselves, instead of binding them to Christ. "Here is where the humanly strong person is in his element, securing for himself the admiration, the love, or the fear of the weak. . . . [This] appears in all forms of conversion wherever the superior power of one person is consciously or unconsciously misused to influence profoundly and draw into his spell another individual or a whole community."[19] Often the *seelisch*, humanly strong person is the minister herself or himself. And the church is only a club.

The most obvious characteristic of a club is that it serves its own members. It is interested in fulfilling their needs, whether physical or spiritual; providing their recreation, whether physical or spiritual; assuring their development, whether physical or spiritual. Of course a church has services to render to its own members. They have great needs. They are ignorant and must be taught the foundations of faith—Christian education. They are apathetic and must be aroused—preaching. They are bruised and wounded by life and must be healed—pastoral work. They are in each other's way and need organizing—administration. All these ye ought to have done!

The question is, Where is the priority? Where is most of the time of church members spent when they do what they call "church work"? Are they out in the world in the work of proclamation, justice, compassion, and peace? Or are they oiling the ecclesiastical machinery? Examine the church budget. How many dollars go to serve the needs of the world, and how many to maintain the institution of the church? Have we gone out into the world in any meaningful way, or are we still hiding in the sanctuary?

All too often our churches are not transparent. They are terribly opaque, directing attention to their possessions, their achievements, their image, their reputation in the community. So the glory of God cannot shine through them; only the glory they bestow upon themselves. We need to hear that shattering word: "As the Father has sent me, even so I send you." We need to direct our attention to the world about us and its pressing needs. It is true of the church as it is of the individual disciple: only when we lose our life do we truly find it.

3. The Individual Christian: Also Sent

As thou didst send me into the world, so I have sent them into the world. (John 17:18)

We said at the beginning of the previous chapter that the idea of an individualistic religion with no supportive community is foreign to Scripture. That does not mean, however, that the individual is unimportant and has no part to play. Indeed, in the mission of the church to the world, the individual member has the key part to play. For the *gathered* church often has very little direct impact on the world. It is as the individual members of the church permeate all the places of work, of government, of education, as they reach all layers of society, it is as the church is *scattered* that its impact on the world is felt. Individual Christians are the fingers of the body of Christ, touching the world at crucial points.

Just as Jesus finds his identity in having been

sent into the world, just as the church finds its identity in having been sent by Christ, so the individual Christian is identified as one who is sent. We said in the Introduction that one of the verbs for "send" is *apostellō*. The noun for "sent one" is *apostolos*, from which we get our word "apostle." It has often been noticed that the Fourth Gospel uses *apostolos* only once, and then not as a title for the "twelve apostles."[20] This is because we are *all* apostles, all sent ones, all missionaries.

This raises resistance immediately, for "missions" has always been a minority hobby among Christians, and "missionaries" have been a small and special group. Does it mean that all of us should go to out-of-the-way places? Some of us should. More of us than do now. The least it can mean is that all of us should live, in whatever place we are, seeking the will of God, and the words of God, and the works of God, and the life that comes from God, because Christ has sent us to that very place in the world. We should be transparent so the glory of God can shine through us.

WHAT MAKES A CHRISTIAN A CHRISTIAN?

In this instance, our theological resistance may be as strong as our practical resistance. It calls for uncomfortable theological rethinking, for some disturbance of Chalcedonian orthodoxy, to say that what makes Christ Christ is his sense of having been sent. And it calls for more uncomfortable rethinking, for some disturbance of the traditional marks of the church, to say that what makes the church the church is its having been sent by Christ. But to say that what makes a Christian a Christian is this same sending disturbs us in the part of theology with which we are most familiar and which we are apt to regard as most essential. It calls for a rethinking of faith and works, of justification and sanctification. It would suggest that to the familiar chapters of the Westminster Confession on Effectual Calling, Justification, Adoption, Sanctification, Saving Faith, Repentance Unto Life, Good Works, Perseverance, and Assurance, a chapter on Being Sent should be added, and that that chapter would be in some sense more basic than the others.

Toward the end of his massive *Church Dogmatics*, Karl Barth wrestles with the question: What makes the Christian a Christian?[21] Characteristically, it takes him many pages to work it out. But he says something which is well worth pondering, and which seems to me to fit precisely with what the Gospel of John says.

Barth looks at two answers that are traditionally given to this question. One we may call the works answer: A Christian is one who observes a certain standard of conduct; who does certain things and does not do certain other things. There is much truth in this answer. Faith without works is dead. By their fruits you shall know them. There is a Christian quality of life and action. To quote Barth: "No discussion of the antithesis between Moses and Christ or the Law and the Gospel should cause us to overlook or even contest the fact that in his relationship with Christians as His own Jesus Christ is their Commander, their supreme and indeed true and only Lawgiver, with a power and authority incomparably greater than that of Moses. The particularity in which Christians stand at the side of God in and in face of the world consists quite indisputably in the rendering of the obedience of life which they owe Him as their Lord."[22]

Yet there are problems in making this the answer to what makes a Christian a Christian. For one thing, in actuality there are practitioners of other religions and there are good humanists who achieve levels of moral conduct that put many Christians to shame. The distinctive thing about Christian morality is not how well Christians do it, but why they do it. To quote Barth again: "The Christian ethos does not allow itself to be understood as an end in itself. It is not a first thing, but follows from what ... He who commands and they who obey are in themselves and in their mutual relationship prior to their commanding and obedience."[23]

The other traditional answer may be called the grace answer: a Christian is one who has received the grace of Christ, who has been forgiven and renewed, who enjoys the benefits won on the cross. Of course there is much truth in this answer. It is the classic answer to which most of the Christian creeds and confessions testify. Barth startles us by questioning its right to be the final answer just as he questioned the right of the works answer. Once again, we are confronted by non-Christians who at least seem to enjoy, in some cases to an astonishing degree, something of the same peace and patience and trust and discipline and freedom that are usually reckoned among the benefits of Christ. A more disturbing problem is the temptation to moral irresponsibility that has always haunted this answer. If the heart of being a Christian is to know that Jesus paid it all, is there really a reason for moral earnestness and obedience? Most disturbing of all is the possible selfishness of this position. Christ is one who gives, but the Christian is one who gets. To quote Barth again: "Does not this wholly possessive being seem to smack of the sanctioning and cultivating of an egocentricity which is only too human for all its sanctity, of a self-seeking which in the light of what is at stake renders every other form of self-seeking quite innocuous?"[24]

Barth then turns to Scripture and surveys all the accounts there of people who became Christians. None of the conversions is of the type we encounter in Augustine, or in testimony meetings today: "First I didn't look for salvation. Then I tried to find it in the wrong place. Finally I found it in the right place." They are all of the Paul type: "Rise and stand upon your feet; for I have appeared to you for this purpose, to appoint you to serve and bear witness to the things in which you have seen me and to those in which I will appear to you, delivering you from the people and from the Gentiles—to whom I send you to open their eyes, that they may turn from darkness to light and from the power of Satan to God, that they may receive forgiveness of sins and a place among those who are sanctified by faith in me" (Acts 26:16–18).

In short, the experience that makes a person a Christian is the experience in which Christ sends that person, gives that person a mission. The great personal benefits of our own forgiveness and salvation are given us in order that we may open the eyes of others. And the commandments of Christ are issued us as our marching orders for the mission. The works answer and the grace answer both make sense as part of the mission answer. Barth says that where the creeds and confessions speak of the state of grace and salvation of the called, "Scripture always speaks of the commissioning and sending of the called man, and sees him set in a function to be exercised between God . . . and the world."[25] In its exercise the called one's own salvation is surely important. "But the principle which controls the structure of his existence as one who is called is that God on the one side and the world . . . on the other have become more important to him . . . than he can be to himself."[26] One thinks of David Livingstone when the pious lady inquired about his soul. "Soul, madam? To tell the truth I've been so concerned about Africa I forgot I had a soul!"

To be a Christian is to be sent on Christ's mission. And being good and being saved are subsidiary to being sent!

THE IMITATION OF CHRIST

We said in Chapter 1 that a missionary Christology reopens the possibility of the imitation of Christ. A missionary understanding of the Christian individual seizes that possibility.

Remember how Jesus used to stop and take time with people who interrupted him and upset his plans, because maybe God was sending him to those people that day? Remember how he never let the future tighten him up so he could not live to the hilt in the present moment, because he felt God had sent him into that very present situation? Remember how in the tightest spot he never felt completely alone because "He who sent me is with me" (John 8:29)? This life-style is a possibility for individual Christians.

In a world of competition, ambition, assertiveness training, individual Christians can imitate Christ by seeking not their own will, but the will of the One who sent them.

In a world of words, high-speed presses, instant copies, junk mail, endless broadcasts, Christians can imitate Christ by speaking not their own words but the words of the One who sent them.

In a world where we hear more than we can take in, we can break free from the constant bombardment of the media, the noise pollution, and imitate Christ by paying strict attention to the voice of the One who sends us.

In a world of business and busyness, where there is too much work for some and too little for others, the Christians can imitate Christ by doing the works of the One who sent them. And for this imitation there is an astounding promise: "Truly, truly, I say to you, he who believes in me will also do the works that I do; and greater works than these will he do, because I go to the Father" (John 14:12).

In a world where the television screen constantly reminds us that a person's life consists in the abundance of things that he possesses, Christians can imitate Christ who had nowhere to lay his head, but who drew his life from the One who sent him.

If being sent involved humiliation and suffering

for him, it will involve some of the same for us. If we reject lowly service to the most material needs of people as authentic mission, as that to which we are sent, then we cannot claim to be sent by the One who took the basin and the towel. It was in that precise connection that he called us all apostles (see above). If we insist that Christian discipleship must be noncontroversial, stirring up no opposition from the established order, then we can hardly claim that Jesus sent us: "If the world hates you, know that it has hated me before it hated you. If you were of the world, the world would love its own; but because you are not of the world, but I chose you out of the world, therefore the world hates you. Remember the word that I said to you, 'A servant is not greater than his master.' If they persecuted me, they will persecute you; if they kept my word, they will keep yours also. But all this they will do to you on my account, because they do not know him who sent me" (John 15:18–21). If we use our position as Christians, whether we are pastors, Sunday school teachers, officers, or anything else, to call attention to ourselves, to gain power over people and manipulate them and bind them to ourselves, then we can hardly claim to have been sent by the One who was utterly transparent and who said: "He who believes in me, believes not in me but in him who sent me" (12:44).

THE GLORY OF DISCIPLESHIP

Being sent is the source of Christ's glory, as well as of his transparency. It is the source of the church's glory. And it is the source of the glory of the individual Christian.

Raymond E. Brown calls John 13–20 "The Book of Glory."[27] Not only the glory of Jesus is shown here, but, especially in chs. 13–17, the glory of the disciples.

They are his own, who are loved (John 13:1, 34). He calls them no longer servants, but friends (15:15). They have a oneness with him. Again, not an equation between two nouns, but a dynamic, missionary oneness, like the oneness of the Father and the Son. "If a man loves me, he will keep my word, and my Father will love him, and we will come to him and make our home with him" (14:23). "Abide in me, and I in you" (15:4). "Even as thou, Father, art in me, and I in thee, that they may also be in us" (17:21). To them is given the promise of answered prayer: "Whatever you ask in my name, I will do it, that the Father may be glorified in the Son; if you ask anything in my name, I will do it" (14:13–14; see 15:7; 16:23). In being sent, there is peace (14:27; 16:33) and joy (15:11; 16:24). In the chain of mission, the individual disciple even becomes the test of faith: "Truly, truly, I say to you, he who receives any one whom I send receives me; and he who receives me receives him who sent me" (13:20).

One of the great promises to the disciples is the coming of the Holy Spirit, the Paraclete. Before analyzing those passages in detail, we must consider something which we can delay no longer: the world, into which Jesus was sent, and the church is sent, and the individual Christian is sent.

4. The World: Into Which We Are Sent

I have given them thy word; and the world has hated them because they are not of the world, even as I am not of the world. (John 17:14)

Be of good cheer, I have overcome the world. (John 16:33)

Behold, the Lamb of God, who takes away the sin of the world! (John 1:29)

We have said that Jesus' sense of having been sent into the world illuminates the ineffable mystery of who he is. We have said that being sent into the world is perhaps the essential mark which defines the church. We have said that the Christian individual may best be defined, not as the one who obeys and does good, or as the one who receives grace, but as the one who is commissioned by God for service in the world.

In all this we have not said very much about what the world is. Service to the world is something beyond service to one's self, the church is more than a club—that much is clear. But what is the world?

The word which is translated "world" throughout John is *kosmos*, which is simply transliterated into our English word "cosmos." Cosmos is the opposite of chaos, and inherent in the word is the idea of order, structure, system. It is clearly a technical term in the Johannine writings, occurring 78 times in the Gospel and 24 times in the epistles. As the article in Kittel's *Wordbook* says, *kosmos* is "at the center of John's theological thinking in a way not true elsewhere in the New Testament."[28]

Kosmos is occasionally a synonym for *ta panta*, all things, the entire universe in its order and structure. (Compare the comprehensive phrase of the Old Testament: "the heavens and the earth.") Thus John 1:2: "All things were made through him"; John 1:10: "The world was made through him." Or again, it may mean all people, the entire human race. John 12:19: "Look, the world *(kosmos)* has gone after him"; John 12:32: "And I, when I am lifted up from the earth, will draw all men *(pantas)* to myself."

HUMAN SOCIETY STRUCTURED IN OPPOSITION TO CHRIST

Most often, in John, *kosmos* refers to human society as it is structured in opposition to Christ and to the followers of Christ. In the references at the head of this chapter we can quickly sense the hatred of the world for Christ and his followers, the struggle of Christ against the world, the world's need of redemption.

It is this meaning of "world," almost normative in John, that is most useful in understanding our contemporary world. What is the world in which we live? The usual analysis consists of a string of adjectives: the world come of age, the secular world, technological, urban, bureaucratic, materialistic, narcissistic. Or there are metaphors that have become common parlance: spaceship earth, the global village. All of these are helpful, but to understand our mission in the world we need to see it as a series of ordered, structured, interlocking systems that are actually and potentially destructive of human values of the most basic kind and are therefore opposed to God who is the source of such values.

Racial segregation is such a system. If we look at it, we shall know what "the world" is. It is found almost everywhere and it is terribly destructive of human beings and human values. But the more ordered and structured it is, the more destructive it is. Just now it approaches the height of order and system in the *apartheid* system of South Africa.

The black people whose labor has built the gleaming cities of that land, who keep their streets and sidewalks so neat, their shrubbery properly pruned, their houses and offices cleaned, their tennis courts rolled and lined, do not for the most part live in the cities. They live in all-black "townships." In the township that I saw, there are mercury vapor lamps, which, should there be a nighttime uprising, can be turned up by the authorities to blinding intensity. But despite the presence of all that voltage in the area, most homes are without electricity. There are as many as 14 people to a room, 42 people in a small house. People struggle to keep clean in the mud and filth of back alleys.

The authorities will explain to you that there is no point in improving the townships, because the townships are temporary. When the Grand Design is complete, no one will live in townships. All blacks will live in their "homelands," enclaves of the most arid and useless land. Those whose labor is useful will "enter South Africa" as "foreign workers." They will live in barracks, called "hostels," away from their families for six months at a time. Since they will be aliens who enter South Africa only to sell their labor, they will have no civil or political rights whatsoever. They can claim their rights in their homelands. There are already hostels in operation. And already the families of the men in the hostels have been removed to the homelands. The Grand Design is under way.

Many white South Africans, and many British and Americans doing business in South Africa, will tell you that, though the system is inhuman, it is bound to benefit everybody in the long run. As the 4½ million whites grow richer and richer, some of that wealth is bound to trickle down and improve the lot of the 26 million blacks. But, the ecologists tell us, South Africa, for all its size and beauty and resources, could not possibly support 30 million people on the scale on which the whites presently live. The amount of consumable goods cannot be produced. And, if it could, the resulting pollution would be more than the land could bear. The standard of living of South Africa's blacks can be improved only by simplifying the life-style of the whites and reducing their affluence.

And that is a parable of the world. On a world scale, we in the United States, in Western Europe, and Japan, may be compared to the 4½ million affluent whites of South Africa. And the people of the Southern Hemisphere, plus considerable pockets in the Northern Hemisphere, may be compared to South Africa's 26 million poor and powerless blacks. And this planet, for all its size and beauty and resources, could not possibly support its billions on the scale on which we live. The lot of the wretched of the earth can be improved only by simplifying our life-style and reducing our affluence.

Now this is nothing new. We've been told this over and over again. But we seem unable to hear it, and certainly unable to do anything about it. On a planet structured graciously by God, the dehumanizing structures that we have made, and in which we are trapped, roll on and on, grinding people to bits. That's the world into which Christ was sent, into which the church is sent, into which you and I are sent day by day.

Militarism is another such structure. No sane person wants to see the nuclear shoot-out between superpowers which will kill hundreds of millions of human beings and leave a great portion of our planet in ruins. In fact, few people can really seriously imagine that it will happen. It is quite literally unthinkable. Yet again and again attempts to put a cap on the arms race, to slow it down, are roundly defeated and serious *dis*armament is not considered at all.

Ordinarily kind and thoughtful people call for increased military expenditures because, although we are reportedly able to sustain a first strike and to retaliate by destroying all the major Russian cities six times over, we suspect that the Russians can now sustain a first strike and retaliate by destroying all the major American cities eight times over. We are no longer Number One! We must catch up at all costs.

Mathematically speaking, 6 times 0 is 0; and 8 times 0 is 0; and 0 is not more or less than 0. Humanly speaking, those kind and thoughtful people are talking about the deaths of hundreds of millions of children, old people, women, and men —sick people burned alive in their beds, mothers annihilated nursing their babies, children pulverized in the schoolroom, works and monuments of human genius reduced to instant ashes, the good earth rendered poisonous and untillable, the fabric of civilization so utterly torn asunder that, as one of the generals said, "the survivors will envy the dead."

This is nothing new either. We've been told this over and over again. But we seem unable to hear it, certainly unable to do anything about it. On this bright blue ball floating in the blackness of space, structured by God as the gracious place where human life can be supported, the dehumanizing structures which we have made and in which we are trapped seem to move us relentlessly toward an unthinkable holocaust. That's the world, into which Christ was sent, into which the church is sent, into which you and I are sent day by day.

RELIGIOUS LEADERS: A "TYPE" OF THE WORLD

Before proceeding to an analysis of what the Johannine missionary theology says about the world in this sense, it will be wise to detour to the vexed subject of John's treatment of "the Jews." For I agree with Bultmann on this point, that "the Jews" are a murky and unexpected synonym for the world. They are, says Bultmann, the representatives of unbelief and thereby of the unbelieving world in general.[29]

The Fourth Gospel is an embarrassment because of its apparent anti-Semitism. According to the usual account, the Synoptics make it clear that only a tiny fraction of the Jewish people, certain parties and leaders, were responsible for accusing Jesus to the Romans; but John, by lumping everyone under the endlessly repeated term "the Jews," unjustly places the guilt on the whole nation.

A careful reading, however, makes it clear that not all of the Jewish people are meant by "the Jews." The people are often more open to Jesus than the authorities, reminding us of the Synoptic accounts. Thus, some of the people said: "He is a good man" (7:12); "Can it be that the authorities really know that this is the Christ?" (7:26); "When the Christ appears, will he do more signs than this man?" (7:31); "This is really the prophet" (7:40); "This is the Christ" (7:41). At this point John places on the lips of some of the Jewish people the confession that the Synoptics reserve for the apostle Peter alone! Of course, others of the people did not believe. There was a division of the people over him (7:43). Sometimes John blurs the distinction between the people and "the Jews," as when "the Jews" of 7:15 become "the people" of 7:20. But in the main it is clear enough that "the Jews" does not mean the entire Jewish people.

"The Jews" appears at times to be a code word for the Pharisees, as in 1:19 and 1:24; 4:1 and 3:25; 18:3 and 18:12. But this is not carried through consistently. The two groups are clearly distinct in 11:45–46, where some of "the Jews" went and told the Pharisees about the raising of Lazarus. The water is further muddied by statements that the Pharisees were divided over Jesus (9:16) and that many of "the Jews" believed in him, at least for a time (8:30–31).

John, we may say, is not anti-Semitic in the sense of condemning the whole Jewish people outright. But he clearly reflects an intense Christian-Jewish conflict. Raymond Brown suggests that the conflict which colors the Johannine narrative occurred in the last decade of the first century and is "read back" into the time of Jesus.[30] After A.D. 90 the Pharisees were the sole surviving party among the Jews, and the main argument between Jews and Christians centered, not on the law as in Jesus' day, but on the Christian claims that Jesus was Messiah and Son of God. The Jewish-Christian confrontation had hardened; Jews who accepted Jesus as Messiah were expelled from the synagogue.[31]

Let us pause here to state clearly that whatever conflict may have occurred toward the end of the first century furnishes no excuse for anti-Semitism in our day or for failure to pursue the avenues for Jewish-Christian dialogue that have been so graciously opened to us.

What we can learn from this early and unfortunate conflict between religious groups is that worldliness reaches its highest point and finds its greatest demonstration among religious leaders. It is religious people, Reinhold Niebuhr reminds us, who commit the most cruel, destructive, and devastating sins.

In the bitter dialogues with Jesus, what we hear is not a racial voice or a national voice. It is the voice of the world's religious people, among whom we must number ourselves.

Religious people ask for signs (John 2:18; 6:30), object to the breaking of rules (5:10; 7:23; 9:16), slander their opponents: "You are a Samaritan and have a demon" (8:48), excommunicate those who raise honest questions (9:34). Religious people misunderstand. How many of the dialogues between Jesus and his opponents arise out of a misunderstanding of what he has said! "Destroy this temple," says Jesus, speaking of his body, but they think he speaks of Herod's temple (2:19–22). "You must be born anew," says Jesus to Nicodemus, speaking of spiritual rebirth; but Nicodemus can only think of reentering his mother's womb (3:3–8). "I am the bread of life," says Jesus; and his opponents dispute among themselves: "How can this man give us his flesh to eat?" (6:25–59). "I go to him who sent me," says Jesus, "you will seek me and you will not find me"; "Where does this man intend to go?" the religious leaders ask, "to ... the Greeks? Will he kill himself?" (7:33–36; 8:21–22). "You will know the truth, and the truth will make you free," says Jesus; "We are descendants of Abraham and have never been in bondage to anyone," they reply (8:31–33). Jesus sums it up: "Why do you not understand what I say? It is because you cannot bear to hear my word" (8:43).

The Johannine Jesus has stern things to say about religious people. He says that they have never heard or seen God (John 5:37). "You do not

have his word abiding in you" (5:38). "You have
not the love of God within you" (5:42). "You . . .
do not seek the glory that comes from the only
God" (5:44). They do not believe Moses (5:47).
"None of you keeps the law" (7:19). "You judge
according to the flesh" (8:15). "You will die in your
sins" (8:24). "You are of your father the devil"
(8:44). They have not known God (8:55).

He really knew how to hurt a religious person,
didn't he? So, again and again, they sought to kill
him, they tried to arrest him, they took up stones
to stone him, they put out a contract on him, and
they finally did him in. Jesus knew all along who
they were: "You are from below, . . . you are of
this world" (John 8:23).

The terror of the South African situation is the
support of *apartheid* by the Dutch Reformed
Church. That is where the world reaches the peak
of worldliness. The horror of the grip of the indus-
trial-military complex upon us is the jingoistic
support it receives from powerful religious voices
that fill our airwaves and dominate our television
screens. That is where the world is really the
world.

A THEOLOGICAL ANALYSIS OF THE WORLD

Now to formulate a theological analysis of the
world into which we are sent.

First, it is a *blind world.* "He was in the world,

and the world was made through him, yet the world knew him not" (John 1:10). "O righteous Father, the world has not known thee" (17:25). As we have seen, the blindness of the world peaks among religious people. The continual inability of "the Jews" to understand what Jesus was driving at is a major demonstration of the world's blindness. The story of the blind man in ch. 9, then, is of focal theological importance. Listen to its conclusion:

> Jesus said: "For judgment I came into this world, that those who do not see may see, and that those who see may become blind." Some of the Pharisees near him heard this, and they said to him, "Are we also blind?" Jesus said to them, "If you were blind, you would have no guilt; but now that you say, 'We see,' your guilt remains." (John 9:39–41)

The world, personified in its religious leaders, is blind in a deep and culpable sense. John brings the first half of his book, the public ministry of Jesus, to a close with a theological meditation on Isa. 53:1 and Isa. 6:10. (The latter passage plays a similar role in the Synoptic Gospels.)

> Though he had done so many signs before them, yet they did not believe in him; it was that the word spoken by the prophet Isaiah might be fulfilled:
> "Lord, who has believed our report,
> and to whom has the arm of the
>   Lord been revealed?"

Therefore they could not believe. For Isaiah again said,

>"He has blinded their eyes and
>   hardened their heart,
>lest they should see with their eyes
>   and perceive with their heart,
>   and turn for me to heal them."

Isaiah said this because he saw his glory and spoke of him. Nevertheless many even of the authorities believed in him, but for fear of the Pharisees they did not confess it, lest they should be put out of the synagogue: for they loved the praise of men more than the praise of God. (John 12:37–43)

Willful blindness, the choice not to see! That is what operates in South African *apartheid* and in American and Russian militarism and everywhere in the world.

Second, the world in its blindness *is the enemy* of Christ, the enemy of the church, the enemy of the individual disciple. We are being sent into enemy territory. Jesus said to his brothers: "The world cannot hate you, but it hates me because I testify of it that its works are evil" (John 7:7). To his disciples he said, "If the world hates you, know that it has hated me before it hated you. If you were of the world, the world would love its own; but because you are not of the world, but I chose you out of the world, therefore the world hates you.... If they persecuted me, they will persecute you. . . . But all this they will do to you on my account. . . . He who hates me hates my Father also. . . . They have seen [my works] and hated both me and my Father" (15:18–25).

As we have seen, the enmity of the world peaks among religious people. Their unceasing hatred of Jesus is a major demonstration of the world's hatred. Speak Jesus' clear word from inside the *apartheid* system or from inside the military system and it is the religious leaders who will attack you first.

The world's enmity toward Jesus is enough to make us very cautious about such slogans as "Let the world set the agenda for the church," "holy worldliness," and so on. The secular theology of a decade ago, with its glorification of the secular city and the world come of age, understood accurately the great danger of bad religion, but it forgot that even without religion the world is the enemy of God. The danger of holy worldliness is that we will embrace the world, be conformed to the world. Because the world is the enemy, organized and structured in opposition to God, John is full of warnings that we must observe a critical distance, we cannot be "of the world": The disciples are those "whom thou gavest me out of the world" (John 17:6). "They are not of the world, even as I am not of the world" (17:16).

Third—and here is the news!—the world is *God's beloved enemy.* I could wish that John 3:16 were not so familiar to us, that we might be hearing for the first time that incredible word of grace, that despite its willful blindness and mad hatred,

God loves the world enough to give his Son. The command to love our enemies, says Calvin, is not merely difficult, but utterly against human nature.[32] But God obeys his own difficult command.

Here is the answer to the charge of anti-Semitism. If "the Jews" are, in Bultmann's phrase, the representatives of the unbelieving world in general, and if God loves that unbelieving world to the point of incredible sacrifice, then our duty to love the Jews is clear, as is our duty to love the Dutch Reformed Church and the television preachers and the myopic members of our own congregations.

Fourth, love invades the world as *light.* Here is a very positive use of the imagery later adopted by Gnostics. "In him was life, and the life was the light of men. The light shines in the darkness, and the darkness has not overcome it" (John 1:4–5). "I am the light of the world; he who follows me will not walk in darkness, but will have the light of life" (8:12). "As long as I am in the world, I am the light of the world" (9:5). "I have come as light into the world, that whoever believes in me may not remain in darkness" (12:46).

It is interesting that John does not repeat the Synoptic word: "You are the light of the world" (Matt. 5:14). But if Jesus is sent into the world as light, and if we recall his words "As the Father has sent me, so I send you," the role of the church and of individual Christians as bearers of light is clear enough.

Fifth, light produces *judgment.* The very presence in the world of Jesus, or the church, or the individual Christian, throws the world into a crisis of self-judgment. "This is the judgment, that the light has come into the world, and [people] loved darkness rather than light, because their deeds were evil" (John 3:19; cf. vs. 20 and 21). "For judgment I came into this world, that those who do not see may see, and that those who see may become blind" (9:39).

Perhaps here is the place to deal, if we can, with that mysterious Johannine figure, "the ruler of this world." In its enmity toward God, in its resistance to God's loving gift of light, the cosmos is so organized, so structured, that some kind of manager, director, chief bureaucrat, moderator, ruler of the world is posited. It is upon this ruler that the judgment is concentrated. "Now is the judgment of this world, now shall the ruler of this world be cast out" (John 12:31). "The ruler of this world is coming. He has no power over me" (14:30). "The ruler of this world is judged" (16:11). These passages do not compel us to make belief in a personal devil an article of faith. But the point is a powerful one. God's light throws the world into a crisis of self-judgment, not just on the shabby edges of worldliness, but at its powerful center, where it is educated, suave, polite, and "fiscally responsible."

At the height of the civil rights battle, the year in which the three young men were murdered and buried in a dam in Mississippi, I was sent to Jackson, Mississippi, to teach the book of Ephesians to the Women's Training School of the Synod of Mississippi. I arrived in the evening, and the matron of the dormitory where I was assigned a room called me in and for two hours, without drawing breath, engaged in a defense of segregation, all the old arguments I had known by heart since I was a boy. When she finally paused I said: "If you are so sure of all of this, why have you spent so much time telling me?" She looked at me in silence and then burst into tears. "Because I may be wrong," she said. The weak and flickering light of my presence, a man from faraway Kentucky, had, without a word, thrown her into a crisis of self-judgment.

What if the church by its very presence in the community could produce such a crisis, if people walking by and seeing the steeple were thrown into self-judgment? That is what we are sent into the world to be and do.

Sixth, judgment is not the last word; *salvation* is. "For God sent the Son into the world, not to condemn the world, but that the world might be saved through him" (John 3:17). "I did not come to judge the world but to save the world" (12:47). "We know that this is indeed the Savior of the world" (4:42). The atonement is not absent from John: Christ dies for the salvation of the world. "Behold, the Lamb of God, who takes away the sin of the world!" (1:29). "And I, when I am lifted up

from the earth, will draw all men *(pantas)* to myself" (12:32). Christ's purpose is not the destruc-
tion of the world, the death of the world, but its
life. "The bread of God is that which comes down
from heaven, and gives life to the world. . . . I am
the living bread which came down from heaven; if
any one eats of this bread, he will live for ever;
and the bread which I shall give for the life of the
world is my flesh" (6:33, 51). It is the role of Christ
and Christ's church to lead the world to that
knowledge and to that faith which make its salvation possible. "I do as the Father has commanded
me, so that the world may know that I love the
Father" (14:31). "I do not pray for these only, but
also for those who believe in me through their
word, that they may all be one; even as thou, Father, art in me, and I in thee, that they also may
be in us, so that the world may believe that thou
hast sent me. The glory which thou hast given me
I have given to them, that they may be one even
as we are one, I in them and thou in me, that they
may become perfectly one, so that the world may
know that thou hast sent me and hast loved them
even as thou hast loved me" (17:20–23).

I am often asked a good old pragmatic American question: "What would be the advantages of
the reunion of the churches? Will a reunited
church be more efficient? Will it save money? Will
it work better?" To this I have to reply: "Probably
not." "Why then reunion?" "It is a matter of obedience. The knowledge of the world, the belief of

the world, the salvation of the world are at stake."

This, then, is a Johannine theology of the world. The world is human society structured and ordered against God: blind, hostile, and yet beloved. God's love enters it as light, as judgment, as salvation. This is the world of *apartheid,* of militarism, of all the interlocking systems that destroy human life and human value. This is the world into which Christ was sent, and the church is sent, and you and I are sent day after day.

THE CONTRAST WITH A GNOSTIC VIEW OF THE WORLD

We have one remaining chore, to contrast this theology of the world with Gnosticism. There is no other point at which the contrast is more illuminating. Gnosticism agrees that the world is God's enemy. It is a "world of darkness, utterly full of evil . . . full of devouring fire . . . full of falsehood and deceit . . . a world of turbulence without steadfastness, a world of darkness without light . . . a world of death without eternal life, a world in which the good things perish and plans come to naught."[33] But Gnosticism knows nothing of God's love for the world. God did not create it and does not care for it or intend to save it. The task of the Gnostic redeemer is to rescue out of the dark world the scattered sparks of light that are now entrapped there and lead them back to the Realm of Light. Does that sound familiar? There is a Gnostic kind of evangelism that proposes just such a rescue. As an Oriental Christian described it, it is netting fish out of the dirty river of the world and putting them into the calm, clear pond of the church. Whenever you have the idea that the church is separated from the world, calm, clean, undisturbed, you have Gnosticism. Whenever your object is to get people out of the world, you have Gnosticism. Whenever there is no concern that the world—in all its wrongheaded order, system, and organization—is to be enlightened, judged, and saved, you have Gnosticism. Jesus will not pray that we be taken out of the world (John 17:15). He sends us into the world (17:18). The project is not escape from *apartheid,* militarism, and the rest. The project is redeeming them. Mission in that sense is a tough assignment. We need help. And that is the subject of our next chapter.

5. The Holy Spirit: Sent to Aid Us in Our Mission

> But when the [Paraclete] comes, whom I shall
> send to you from the Father, even the Spirit of
> truth, who proceeds from the Father, he will
> bear witness to me. (John 15:26)

God sent Jesus into the blind and hateful world,
which would not understand him and did him in.
Jesus sends us into the same world. "As thou
didst send me into the world, so I have sent them
into the world" (John 17:18). It is a world that will
not understand us and wants to do us in. We are
not sent into the world to plan and execute the
escape of a few souls, but to bear our witness to
the world as a structured, ordered cosmos, organized in opposition to God. That is a tough assignment. We need help.

We can be grateful that there is one more sending. "But the [Paraclete], the Holy Spirit, whom
the Father will send in my name, he will teach you
all things, and bring to your remembrance all that
I have said to you" (John 14:26). "Nevertheless I
tell you the truth: it is to your advantage that I go

away, for if I do not go away, the [Paraclete] will not come to you; but if I go, I will send him to you" (16:7). Jesus was sent; he sends us; and he sends the Paraclete to us right in the midst of the world.

When Jerome encountered *paraklētos* in these passages, he could find no adequate translation, so he simply transliterated it: Paraclete. I have followed him in his wisdom, because, as we shall see, our customary English translations are inadequate.

The "Paraclete" is a special name for the Holy Spirit, found only in John, and indeed only in the Farewell Discourse of John 14–16. Bultmann has the theory that the Paraclete was not originally the Holy Spirit at all. The Paraclete was the Mandaean Jawar, the Helper, a Gnostic revealer who often takes the place of, or stands beside, Manda dHaije, the chief Revealer. The Evangelist found this figure in his Gnostic source and interpreted it, in the context of the Christian tradition, as the Holy Spirit.[34] All this is subject to question. There is, indeed, even a question whether such a source ever existed. What is certain is that the Evangelist equated the Paraclete with the Holy Spirit, as he specifically says in John 14:26: "The [Paraclete], the Holy Spirit, whom the Father will send in my name." As Raymond Brown says: "The identification of the Paraclete as the Holy Spirit in 14:26 is not an editorial mistake, for the similarities between the Paraclete and the Spirit are found in all the Paraclete passages."[35]

THE DISTINCTIVE MEANING OF PARACLETE

"Paraclete" designates the Holy Spirit, not in the fullness of his work, but in a special function. Attempts to understand what that special function is have usually gone to the verb *parakaleō* and have not been distinguished by notable success.

Parakaleō means, literally, "call alongside." *Paraklētos,* a passive form, suggests one who is called alongside to help, a Helper. Early on, the setting was considered to be forensic, that of a court trial. So the Paraclete is the defense attorney, the "Advocate" of many early translations, or the "Counselor" of the Revised Standard Version. There are indeed passages outside of John where the Holy Spirit appears in the setting of a trial. There is the promise of Jesus, so well attested in the Synoptic tradition: "And when they bring you to trial and deliver you up, do not be anxious beforehand what you are to say; but say whatever is given you in that hour, for it is not you who speak, but the Holy Spirit" (Mark 13:11). There is a parallel in Matthew (Matt. 10:17–20) and two parallels in Luke (Luke 12:11–12; 21:12–15). In Acts we see that promise fulfilled as words are given to Peter (Acts 4:8) and Stephen (Acts 7:55) in their trials before the Sanhedrin. But in John 14–16, the Paraclete, the Holy Spirit in this special function, does not act as advocate or defense attorney for the disciples in trials before the authorities.

Parakaleō means, in many cases, "intercede." If we ignore the passive structure of *paraklētos* and make it somehow active, the translation "Intercessor" becomes possible. Jesus' intercession for his disciples is a Johannine idea, as we see from the great prayer in John 17. In an interesting passage in the First Epistle of John, *paraklētos* is expressly used of Jesus and clearly means "intercessor": "If any one does sin, we have a [*paraklētos*] with the Father, Jesus Christ the righteous" (I John 2:1). Nor is the idea of the Holy Spirit as an intercessor lacking in the New Testament. Who can forget Romans 8, where "the Spirit himself intercedes for us with sighs too deep for words" (Rom. 8:26)? But nowhere in John 14–16 is it said that the Paraclete, the Holy Spirit in this special function, intercedes for the disciples.

Once again, the verb *parakaleō* can mean "comfort," which yields the title Comforter, so familiar from the King James Version. In many ways the Holy Spirit comforts us, not least in bearing witness with our spirit that we are children of God (Rom. 8:16). But nowhere in John 14–16 is it said of the Paraclete, the Holy Spirit in this special function, that he comforts the disciples. We come close in John 14:18: "I will not leave you desolate (literally, orphans)"; but the concluding clause is not "I will send the Paraclete," but "I will come to you." That may, indeed, mean the same thing, as we shall see.

Let us abandon etymology and go to the five Paraclete sayings themselves to see what functions are ascribed to the Paraclete. The Paraclete dwells with the disciples and will be in them (John 14:15–17). The Paraclete will teach the disciples all things and bring to their remembrance all that Jesus has said to them (14:26). The Paraclete will bear witness to Jesus (15:26–27). The Paraclete will prove the world to be wrong (16:7–11). The Paraclete will guide the disciples into all truth, declare to them the things to come, glorify Jesus, take what is his and declare it to them (16:12–14). This would suggest such titles as Companion, Teacher, Witness, Guide, Accuser of the World.

What hits us in the face instantly is that these are appropriate titles for Jesus. He was certainly the disciples' Companion. He was preeminently their Teacher: eight times in John he is called Rabbi, not to mention the climactic Rabboni, my teacher, with which Mary Magdalene greets the risen Lord. He was the Witness to whom the Father, and John the Baptist, and his own works also bear witness, as appears in his long controversy with "the Jews." He was not merely the Guide along the way, but the Way itself (John 14:6). And he was the Accuser of the World, as we saw in the preceding chapter. *The distinctive function of the Paraclete is to do what Jesus did, now that Jesus is going away.*

This suggests that the best translation may be Successor, the one called alongside of the Predecessor, to take his place when he is gone. Raymond Brown is very helpful in suggesting certain Old Testament parallels. Joshua is Moses' successor, standing beside him in order to take his place and carry on his work after he is gone. Elisha is Elijah's successor, carrying on in his stead after he is taken up into heaven.[36]

It is important that we not understand the Successor as the Displacer. In the second-century heresy of Montanism, the Paraclete actually displaced Jesus. According to the teaching of Montanus, Priscilla, and Maximilla, what the Spirit reveals to us makes further study of the teachings of Jesus unnecessary. One of the dangers of the current "charismatic renewal" is that personal, ecstatic experiences will become more important to people than what happened in the time of Jesus. Notice how the Fourth Gospel guards against this. Jesus is not the subordinate forerunner of the Paraclete, as John the Baptist was of Jesus—"He must increase, but I must decrease" (John 3:30). No, the Paraclete is the clearly subordinate Remembrancer of Jesus. He will bring to the disciples' remembrance all that Jesus has said to them (14:26). He will bear witness to Jesus (15:26). He will not speak on his own authority, but whatever he hears from Jesus he will speak

(16:13), just as Jesus did not speak on his own authority, but spoke only what he heard from the Father (7:16; 8:26, 28; 12:49; 14:24; 17:8). He will glorify Jesus (16:14), just as Jesus glorified the Father (17:4). As Jesus was utterly transparent, claiming nothing for himself so that the Father's glory might shine through, so the Paraclete is utterly transparent, claiming nothing for himself so that the glory of Jesus may shine through. The Paraclete no more displaces Jesus than Jesus displaces the Father.

DEVELOPING A MISSIONARY DOCTRINE OF THE HOLY SPIRIT

Just as the sending of Jesus led us to a fresh look at Christology, and the sending of the church led us to a fresh look at ecclesiology, and the analysis of the world into which they were sent led us to reexamine cosmology, so the sending of the Paraclete opens the way for a fresh look at pneumatology.

The time seems ripe for that, since today we find ourselves in the presence of unprecedented interest in the Holy Spirit and in spiritual phenomena, notably the "gifts of the Spirit." There is no need here to detail at length the rise of what is now "old-line" Pentecostalism, around the turn of the century, and the subsequent outbreak of "neo-Pentecostalism," Pentecostal enthusiasm within the so-called mainline churches, following World War II. There is probably no reader who does not have friends who are involved in the "charismatic renewal." Many have probably witnessed the phenomenon of "speaking in tongues," and some may have participated in it.

What is needed, it seems to me, is sober theological analysis that will not, on the one hand, attempt to "quench the Spirit" or treat with contempt those who have been exhilarated by these experiences; nor, on the other hand, accept uncritically that this is indeed the era of the Spirit, a time of extraordinary renewal and awesome delight, following the effusion of the Holy Spirit as a new mighty act of God.[37]

The first thing to be said on the basis of our analysis thus far is that *the Holy Spirit is sent to the church.* All the "you's" in the passages with which we began are plural, and they are clearly collective plurals. It is to the disciples as a band, a community, a church, that the Paraclete will be sent. And it is upon them, assembled in one place on Easter evening, that, in the Johannine record, the Holy Spirit is actually bestowed: "And when he had said this, he breathed on them, and said to them, 'Receive the Holy Spirit' " (John 20:22). Although the circumstances of the bestowal of the Spirit in Acts are markedly different and come almost fifty days later, the corporate emphasis is the same: they were *all* together in *one* place; a sound like rushing wind filled *all* the house;

tongues as of fire rested on *each one* of them; they were *all* filled with the Holy Spirit (Acts 2:1–4).

To the extent that the old Westminster orthodoxy concentrated on the work of the Spirit in the effectual calling, justification, sanctification, saving faith, repentance, good works, perseverance, and assurance of individual believers, like unstrung beads in a box—and to the extent that neo-Pentecostalism concentrates on the reception of the baptism of the Spirit and the gifts of the Spirit by individual believers, like unstrung beads in a box—both are out of line with the principal emphasis of Scripture. As in Chapter 2 we insisted that the church is sent into the world, and individuals are sent secondarily as a part of the church's mission; so here we must insist that the Holy Spirit is given primarily to the church and then secondarily to individuals as members of the church. This is perhaps even clearer in the letters of Paul than in John: "For just as the body is one and has many members, and all the members of the body, though many, are one body, so it is with Christ. For by one Spirit we were all baptized into one body—Jews or Greeks, slaves or free—and all were made to drink of one Spirit" (I Cor. 12:12–13). The author of Ephesians is a model of succinctness: "There is one body and one Spirit" (Eph. 4:4).

The second thing to be said is that *the Holy Spirit is sent to the church for its mission.* It is because the church is itself sent that the Paraclete is sent to it. In the solemn setting of the Easter evening scene, the church's commissioning is immediately followed by its reception of the Holy Spirit. First, the verse on which we put so much weight in Chapter 2: "Jesus said ... 'As the Father has sent me, even so I send you'" (John 20:21). Then: "And when he had said this, he breathed on them, and said to them, 'Receive the Holy Spirit'" (John 20:22). This same conjunction of commissioning and endowment with the Holy Spirit occurs in a familiar passage in Acts: "But you shall receive power when the Holy Spirit has come upon you; and you shall be my witnesses in Jerusalem and in all Judea and Samaria and to the end of the earth" (Acts 1:8).

The Holy Spirit is not a useful tool or adjunct in a mission planned and designed by the church. He is the Lord of the mission. He is the Paraclete, Christ's presence in the church while Christ is absent. As, during the days of his flesh, Christ was not a useful tool in the disciples' mission but their Teacher and Director, so now the Holy Spirit is in charge. Since Christ is not here to send them out, the Holy Spirit becomes the Sender. With this the record in Acts agrees. There the Holy Spirit instigates and blocks and rechannels the mission of the church (Acts 13:2, 51–52; 16:6–10).

If the Holy Spirit is sent to the church primarily for its mission, then any benefits he bestows on the church corporately or on the individuals in it are secondary and instrumental to that mission. The Holy Spirit gives unity and peace to the church, and that is most necessary and most important. But the unity and peace are given to enable the church to get on with its mission, and not to persuade the church to sit back and glory in being unified and peaceful as ends in themselves. The Holy Spirit does regenerate and sanctify and assure individual Christians, just as our confessions of faith remind us. But those things are done in order that the individual may participate in the church's mission, and not to persuade the individual to stick in this thumb and pull out a plum and say, "What a good Christian am I." The Holy Spirit does bestow a variety of gifts, workings, offices on believers. But they are given for use in the church's mission, not for the exaltation or even the "second blessing" of individuals. Therefore any kind of spiritual pecking order, or any low self-image because gifts seem to be lacking, or any pride because gifts seem to be extraordinary, is ruled out. The only question is: Are you using such gifts as have been given you for the mission of the church?

The third thing to be said is that *the Holy Spirit is sent to the church for its mission to the world.* The Holy Spirit has to do with segregation and militarism and all those worldly things. At this point we need to work with the most difficult of the Paraclete sayings, John 16:8–11. It reads this way in the RSV (1971): "And when [the Paraclete]

comes, he will convince the world concerning sin
and righteousness and judgment: concerning sin,
because they do not believe in me; concerning
righteousness, because I go to the Father, and
you will see me no more; concerning judgment,
because the ruler of this world is judged." That,
of course, makes very little sense. We know about
convicting—that's really the word, not the weak
"convince"—we know about convicting people of
sin, but whoever heard of convicting them of (or
concerning) righteousness and judgment? Raymond Brown is helpful in suggesting that *elen-
chein peri* ("convict of") is better translated
"prove ... wrong about."[38] I find that this translation works in many other passages besides this
one. So we would read: "When the Paraclete
comes, he will show the world it is wrong about
sin, and about justice (a better translation here
than righteousness), and about judgment."[39] It is
the work of the Holy Spirit to confront the world
and reverse its wordly values. They don't have the
right idea in South Africa about what sin is: they
strain out gnats (strict censorship of movies) and
swallow camels (Soweto and the Grand Design).
They don't have the right idea in the American
Congress about justice: in order to kill the same
people eight times they exacerbate inflation,
which robs us all, they let our inner cities rot and
our black youth suffer 35 percent unemployment
and our elderly poor freeze in their apartments.
They don't have the right idea anywhere about

judgment: people think it's way off yonder at the end of time, but it's here now, already operating. The Paraclete is sent to confront the world with regard to its false values, its bad theology.

Now just how is the Paraclete going to do that? When Jesus was here he did it by his signs and his discourses and his arguments. But the Paraclete has no body and no mouth and no vocal cords. As the Leader of the church's mission, he must do it through the church. Now here is an interesting twist. When the New Testament preachers told the story of Jesus, that was *kērygma*, proclamation. When they dealt with rules and principles for the church's life, that was *didachē*, teaching. But when they got down to issues, that was *paraklēsis*, exhortation. *Paraklēsis* often means comfort, consolation. We saw that the verb *parakaleō* sometimes means to comfort. But in the passages where *paraklēsis* refers to a message, either written or spoken, it clearly means controversial discourse, designed to change people's minds.[40] So the Paraclete confronts the world through the *paraklēsis* of the church!

The Holy Spirit has business to do with the world, regarding the world's false values and bad theology. This sheds some light on that favorite doctrine of past Presbyterian history: the "spirituality" of the church. According to that doctrine, in order to remain "spiritual" the church should not interfere or meddle with the social, political, economic, military affairs of the world. It should stick to "the gospel," which meant evangelistic *kē-rygma* and in-house *didachē*. But, according to the Johannine missionary theology, if the church is to be spiritual, that is, filled and led by the Holy Spirit, it will find itself in confrontation with the world regarding sin, justice, and judgment. And if it is not in such confrontation, it is not obedient to the Spirit, not carrying out its mission; and its peace and unity, its regeneration and sanctification, its plethora of gifts and graces, are all going to waste.

What disturbs me at times about the charismatic renewal is not the speaking in tongues and other ecstatic phenomena, but the retreat from confrontation with the world. There are an increasing number of exceptions to this and the growing number of socially concerned charismatics may be one of the great movements of the Spirit in our day. But one still hears all too often of former battlers for righteousness who have been "baptized by the Spirit" and have withdrawn from the fray into the warmth of "close spiritual fellowship."

The word is out that seminary campuses are much more "spiritual" these days. Who can fail to rejoice in that? But: "Beloved, do not believe every spirit, but test the spirits to see whether they are of God" (I John 4:1).

It is of God we must speak in our final chapter.

6. The God Who Sends

> The Father who sent me . . . (John 5:23, 37;
> 6:44; 8:18; 12:49; 14:24)
>
> The One who sent me . . . (John 4:34; 5:24, 30;
> 6:38, 39; 7:16, 18, 28, 33; 8:16, 26, 29; 9:4; 12:44;
> 13:20; 15:21)

We have been following the word "send" like a
scarlet thread through the intricate labyrinth of
John. Along the way we have received new light
on our old theology. We have been led to a
reevaluation of our Christology, our ecclesiology,
our cosmology, our pneumatology—all from the
standpoint of mission, of being sent. Now, in the
depths of the labyrinth we come to the holy cham-
ber where God dwells. Is there new light to be
shed on the doctrine of God, on what the theologians call "theology proper"?

Who is God? According to the most ancient
creeds of the church, the answer is: the Creator.
As Langdon Gilkey put it: "The most fundamental
question of religious thought is: who is God—He
in whom we put our trust? And the primary an-

swer in both Bible and creed is: 'He is the maker of the heavens and the earth.' "[41] Some Biblical theologians might disagree, pointing out that the weight of Biblical affirmations rests on God as the Doer of mighty acts, and only secondarily as the Creator. The Shorter Catechism would seem to capture both emphases in Question 8:

> Q. 8. How doth God execute his decrees?
> A. God executeth his decrees in the works of creation and providence.

John knows God as Creator. The affirmation in John 1:3 that all things were made through the Word clearly implies that God is the Creator and the Word is his agent. And John knows God as Doer: "My Father is working still, and I am working" (5:17). But John knows God principally as Sender. Over and over and over again, "send" is the verb of which God is the subject.

Who is God? The Father who sent me into the world, says the Johannine Jesus. God is the initiator of the mission in all its aspects: the Sender of Jesus, the Sender of the church, the Sender of the individual disciple, the Sender of the Holy Spirit. God sends all these into the world of which he is indeed the Creator, but a world now strangely and perversely ordered against him. What are the theological results of this missionary view of God?

THE MODEST SOVEREIGNTY OF GOD

God as Sender veils and withholds his sovereignty, so it will not overwhelm us and crush us. He does not appear in his naked majesty, which we could not endure. In gentleness, in consideration of our weakness, he sends a deputy. He gives us room!

It was the need for room that led Paul Tillich to abandon theism, to depersonalize God into the Ground of Being. As he saw it, if God is personal, if God is another subject, then I will have no room to be myself.

> God as a subject makes me into an object which is nothing more than an object. He deprives me of my subjectivity because he is all-powerful and all-knowing. I revolt and try to make *him* into an object, but the revolt fails and becomes desperate. God appears as the invincible tyrant, the being in contrast with whom all other beings are without freedom and subjectivity. He is equated with the recent tyrants who with the help of terror try to transform everything into a mere object, a thing among things, a cog in the machine they control. He becomes the model of everything against which Existentialism revolted. This is the God Nietzsche said had to be killed because nobody can tolerate being made into a mere object of absolute knowledge and absolute control. This is the deepest root of atheism. It is an atheism which is justified as the

reaction against theological theism and its disturbing implications. It is also the deepest root
of the Existentialist despair and the wide-
spread anxiety of meaninglessness in our period.[42]

There is bound to be a reaction if we think of
God as an overweening Parent—or, as we may
say in these blessed nonsexist days, God as an
overprotective Mother, leaving us no room to
grow, no room to mature, no room to reach adulthood. With her absolute knowledge and absolute
control and her continual pressing upon us of the
chicken soup of grace, this God keeps us her itsy-
bitsy infantile children. In the presence of such a
parent the world cannot come of age.

But in the Johannine missionary theology, theism is possible. God is another subject, but he does
not threaten us and cramp us and impose upon us.
The predictions that God will come in might and
majesty to judge, punish, and control are not
fulfilled. God does not come; God sends. God main-
tains distance and gives us room to accept or reject, to make mistakes and learn from them, to
grow, to reach adulthood and maturity. Only a
human parent whose children have grown up can
know the cost and pain and self-discipline involved
in maintaining that distance.

God does not come; God sends a deputy. And
the deputy is—one of us: one who, as we saw in
Chapter 1, bled human blood, spat human spit,
asked human questions, wept human tears, felt

the agony of human thirst, died a human death. This is important for what it tells us about Jesus, but it is even more important for what it tells us about God the Sender. Donald M. Baillie knew this long ago, when he said we have to have a Christology, because without a Christology we teach the wrong things about God.[43]

The Johannine missionary theology is marked by modesty. There is the modesty of Jesus, who claims nothing for himself. His words and deeds are not his own. He is completely transparent to the Father's glory. There is the modesty of the church, which exists not to serve itself, like a fine club, but to confront and serve the world. There is the extreme modesty of the Holy Spirit, who has no face or character of his own, but only points to Jesus, holds up the mirror to Christ's face, serves as the Lord's Remembrancer. And now we have come to the modesty of God, who will not come, who stays at a distance lest he cramp and threaten us, who only sends, and sends one of us.

The Fountain of the Trinity

It is generally acknowledged that the Trinity is not a Biblical doctrine; that is, it is not clearly and formally laid out in the Bible itself. It is certainly not to be found in the Fourth Gospel. It is an attempt, a necessary one, to try to pull together in some kind of logical construct all the varied

Biblical data regarding the Father, the Son, and the Holy Spirit.

The Johannine emphasis on God as Sender points strongly to the medieval idea of God as *fons trinitatis*, the fountain of the Trinity. In working with the Trinity, theologians neglect this to their peril. It may be necessary to insist on the coeternity of the three Persons, as the Westminster Confession does (II. 3). After all, the Son and the Holy Spirit are not creatures. But we must not lose sight of the Father as the Originator, the Initiator, the Sender. It may be necessary to insist on the equality of the three Persons, as the Shorter Catechism does (Question 6). After all, the Son and the Holy Spirit are not second-class, semidivine beings. But we must not lose sight of the real subordination of the Son to the Father (see above, pp. 30–34) and of the Holy Spirit to the Son (see above, pp. 93–94).

One of the most famous Trinitarian controversies relates directly to the Johannine theology of God the Sender: the *filioque* controversy that divided the church between East and West in the eleventh century. The question was whether in the Nicene Creed we say "I believe in the Holy Spirit, the Lord and Giver of Life, who proceeds from the Father"—as the East has always said it; or whether we add "who proceeds from the Father *and the Son*"— as the West had come to say it.

The West, it seems to me, was eager to affirm

the whole Paraclete idea. Whatever else the Holy Spirit may have been and done in the creation of the world and in the inspiration of Israel's judges, kings, prophets, and artisans, in the conception of Jesus and in his empowerment for ministry, once the mission of Jesus to the world was accomplished, the Holy Spirit became the Spirit of Christ, the Paraclete, Jesus' Successor who carries on his work, the presence of Christ in the church while Christ himself is absent. The Holy Spirit proceeds from the Son.

The East, it seems to me, was eager to guard God's role as Sender. It feared the beginning of a chain that might get longer and longer: the Father sends the Son, the Son sends the Spirit, the Spirit sends the apostles, the apostles send the bishops, and on and on. Gnosticism was full of such chains, and used them to separate God at an infinite distance from the world. The Fourth Gospel is really very careful to guard against such a chain, always making the sending by Christ a sending by the Father as well: "The Holy Spirit, whom the Father will send in my name" (John 14:26); "The Paraclete . . . whom I shall send you from the Father, even the Spirit of truth, who proceeds from the Father" (15:26). God remains clearly and always the Sender.

We said earlier that the Johannine Christology is a Christology of verbs rather than nouns. So here the doctrine of the Trinity to which John points is verbal: not the familiar diagram of three circles joined in a triangle—static *things*, sitting there for all eternity—but a movement, a going forth, a sending, a mission. The Trinitarian movement does not turn back on itself, forming a never-ending circle; it is directed toward the world. Faith in the strong name of the Trinity does not involve the believer in endless speculation and static contemplation; it involves a movement into the world, reflecting, imitating, corresponding to, that movement which is the secret of the inner being of the Triune God.

GOD'S INVOLVEMENT IN HUMANITY

God the Sender sounds a bit Gnostic. Even though God's sending remains fairly direct, not at the end of an endless chain, is he not an aloof God, far away in some remote, eternal bliss, awaiting without desire or passion the return of the scattered bits of light that were once parts of his own being? No, that is not the picture, because God is Lover as well as Sender.

The Sender loves the One he has sent. "As the Father has loved me, so have I loved you," says Jesus to the disciples (John 15:9). And he prays "that the world may know that thou hast sent me and hast loved them even as thou hast loved me" (17:23). As everyone who has ever loved knows, we become involved with those whom we love. A detached sending, as one would send over the plumber, becomes impossible. The word "giving" begins to slip in to replace the word "sending." "God so loved the world that he gave his only Son" (3:16). "My Father gives you the true bread from heaven" (6:32). "I will pray the Father, and he will give you another [Paraclete], to be with you for ever" (14:16). There is a note of sacrificial involvement in giving that was not necessarily present in sending. But it does not end there. The Sender's love for the One sent is so great that the giving is an accompanying, a going with.

God does come after all, not in his naked power which would cramp and threaten us, but clothed in the meekness of Jesus.

> Philip said to him, "Lord, show us the Father, and we shall be satisfied." Jesus said to him, "Have I been with you so long, and yet you do not know me, Philip? Whoever has seen me has seen the Father; how can you say, 'Show us the Father'? Do you not believe that I am in the Father and the Father in me?" (John 14:8–10)

> I am not alone, for the Father is with me. (16:32)

> Even as thou, Father, art in me, and I in thee. (17:21)

It must be remembered that this loving, coming with, and mutual indwelling is between God and a bleeding, spitting, thirsting, dying human being. As we have seen, it involves God in loving his

enemy, the world of humanity, structured and organized against him. It involves, in Bonhoeffer's
phrase, "God's sufferings at the hands of a god-
less world."[44] It involves the true and meaningful
death of God. The Johannine missionary theology
in its own way spells out Paul's flash of insight:
"In Christ God was reconciling the world to himself, not counting their trespasses against them"
(II Cor. 5:19).

What we are dealing with here is "the humanity
of God," which constituted such a turning point in
the theological development of Karl Barth. Barth
began as a pretty good Gnostic, with his "infinite,
qualitative difference between time and eternity,"
his "divine No on all that smacks of the human,"
his revelation "direct from above." But when he
came to see Jesus as the Elect Human Being, and
saw election as the decisive turning of God toward
humanity in which God elects the human race as
his people and elects himself to be humanity's
God, so that he no longer wills to be at all except
with his human partner—then he was able to talk
about the God of the Fourth Gospel, the Sender
and Lover.[45]

We set out to recover our sense of mission in a
day of selfish emphasis on survival and escape.
We have seen that the Fourth Gospel is per-
meated with the idea of sending, mission.

The Gnosticism with which this Gospel is in
some way in dialogue and disagreement is pre-

cisely a nonmissionary religion, a religion of survival and escape. The Gnostic communities have no mission to the world. The Gnostic believers have no concern about the surrounding society. The Gnostic creed is, in modern parlance: "Stop the world, I want to get off." Present nonmissionary trends in the church are leading us back to the most ancient of heresies.

If we will take the Fourth Gospel seriously, we will be propelled into mission to the world, in all its ordered, systematic opposition to God. And we will be compelled to rethink our traditional systems of theology in new, creative, missionary ways.

Browning was right on target after all. We are all Gigadibs, in desperate need of a new start:

—there, I hope,
By this time he has tested his first plough,
And studied his last chapter of Saint John.

A Closing Meditation

What does it mean that the blind man, whose story is so focal in this mysterious Gospel of John, is sent to wash in the pool of Siloam, "which means Sent" (John 9:7)? Siloam can possibly be derived from the Hebrew word for "send," but it wrenches language beyond limits to make it mean "Having-been-sent," which is what the Greek says here.

Is John the Theologian doing the same kind of thing here that old John Bunyan did? Is the Pool of Having-been-sent the same kind of place as the Slough of Despond and the Hill called Clear and the Valley of Humiliation and the Delectable Mountains?

If we should wash in the Pool of Having-been-sent, would our eyes be opened? Would we be rid of our illusions, able to see the world as it really is and ourselves as we really are? And would it get us into trouble with the authorities? Would those religious leaders in whom "the world" comes to its final focus cast us out?

In spite of this risk, will the readers and the writer of this little book love the light enough to let a sense of mission be the center of their lives, the center of their identity as Christians? Will they go and wash in the Pool of Having-been-sent?

Notes

1. For convenience, and without affirming anything about the identity of the unknown writer of the Fourth Gospel, we shall use the customary "John" throughout the book.

2. See F.-M. Braun, *Jean le Théologien* (Paris: J. Gabalda, 1959), p. vii.

3. Rudolf Bultmann, *The Gospel of John* (Westminster Press, 1971), p. 50, n. 2; p. 249, n. 2.

4. The minute we start citing texts from the Fourth Gospel the problem of its excessive use of masculine terms strikes us in the face. Not only do we encounter the abundant Father/Son language, but in the Revised Standard Version we meet the constant "he who" and "him who" to translate the Greek definite article with the participle. "The one who" is just as faithful to the Greek and will be used in the writer's own discussion. Unfortunately, the writer does not have permission to alter direct citations from the RSV text. Let us hope

that the RSV revision in progress will result in language that is less oppressive to sensitized people. Some consolation can be drawn from the fact that the Johannine community clearly gave to women a larger, freer, more important place than did the more mainline or "apostolic" communities in the early church. See Raymond E. Brown, *The Community of the Beloved Disciple* (Paulist Press, 1979), pp. 183–198.

5. Bultmann, *The Gospel of John*, pp. 7–9.

6. Brown, *The Community of the Beloved Disciple*.

7. It is a fact that the earliest known commentary on John was written by Heracleon, a Gnostic. The earliest use of John by mainline Christians is almost at the end of the second century. See Brown, *The Community of the Beloved Disciple*, pp. 147–149.

8. José Comblin, *Sent from the Father* (Orbis Books, 1979), p. 11.

9. Paul Tillich, *Systematic Theology* (University of Chicago Press, 1951–1963), Vol. I, pp. 133–134.

10. Albert Schweitzer, *The Quest of the Historical Jesus* (Macmillan Co., 1955), p. 194.

11. Ibid., pp. 370–371.

12. Tillich, *Systematic Theology*, Vol. I, p. 134.

13. For the relation between the use of I AM by the Johannine Jesus and the secret name of God in the Old Testament, see Raymond E. Brown, *The Gospel According to John*, Vol. I, The Anchor Bible, Vol. 29 (Doubleday & Co., 1966), pp. 533–538.

14. John Calvin, *The Institutes of the Christian Religion*, II. 14. 1, 2.

15. The Westminster Confession of Faith, I. 1.

16. "A Declaration of Faith" (Presbyterian Church U.S., 1977), VIII. 1.

17. Karl Barth, *Dogmatics in Outline* (Philosophical Library, 1949), p. 143.

18. Calvin, *The Institutes of the Christian Religion*, IV. 1. 9.

19. Dietrich Bonhoeffer, *Life Together* (Harper & Brothers, 1954), pp. 32–33.

20. The reference is John 13:16: "Truly, truly, I say to you, a servant [properly, slave] is not greater than his master; nor is he who is sent *(apostolos)* greater than he who sent him *(tou pempsantos auton)*."

21. Karl Barth, *Church Dogmatics*, Vol. IV, Part Three, Second Half (Edinburgh: T. and T. Clark, 1962), par. 71, sec. 4 (pp. 554–614).

22. Ibid., p. 559.

23. Ibid., p. 560.

24. Ibid., p. 567.

25. Ibid., p. 592.

26. Ibid.

27. Raymond Brown, *The Gospel According to John*, Vol. II, The Anchor Bible, Vol. 29A (Doubleday & Co., 1970), pp. 539ff.

28. Gerhard Kittel and Gerhard Friedrich (eds.), *Theological Dictionary of the New Testament*, tr. and ed. by Geoffrey W. Bromiley (Wm. B. Eerdmans Publishing Co., 1964–1976), Vol. III, art. *Kosmos*.

29. Bultmann, *The Gospel of John*, p. 86.

30. Brown, *The Gospel According to John*, Vol. I, pp. lxx–lxxv.

31. John 9:22; 12:42; 16:2.

32. Calvin, *The Institutes of the Christian Religion*, III. 7. 6.

33. Quoted in Hans Jonas, *The Gnostic Religion*, 2d ed. (Beacon Press, 1963), p. 57.

34. Bultmann, *The Gospel of John*, pp. 566–572.

35. Brown, *The Gospel According to John*, Vol. II, p. 1140.

36. Ibid., p. 1138.

37. See J. Rodman Williams, *The Era of the Spirit*

(Logos International, 1971).

38. Brown, *The Gospel According to John*, Vol. II, pp. 703–705.

39. *The Jerusalem Bible* offers a striking translation of John 16:8:

"And when he comes,
he will show the world how wrong it was,
about sin,
and about who was in the right,
and about judgment."

40. *Paraklēsis* refers to a spoken message in Acts 13:15; Rom. 12:8; I Thess. 2:3; I Tim. 4:13. It refers to a written message in Acts 15:31; Heb. 12:5; 13:22.

41. Langdon Gilkey, *Maker of Heaven and Earth* (Doubleday & Co., 1959), p. 15.

42. Paul Tillich, *The Courage to Be* (Yale University Press, 1952), p. 185.

43. Donald M. Baillie, *God Was in Christ* (Charles Scribner's Sons, 1948), p. 66.

44. Dietrich Bonhoeffer, *Letters and Papers from Prison*, enlarged ed. (Macmillan Co., 1971), p. 361 (18 July 1944).

45. See Karl Barth's wonderful little book *The Humanity of God* (John Knox Press, 1960).